ADVANCES IN
THE STUDY OF ENTREPRENEURSHIP,
INNOVATION, AND ECONOMIC GROWTH

Volume 8 • 1996

THE INNOVATIVE MIDDLE:
POLITICAL AND ECONOMIC FACTORS
AFFECTING MID-SIZE BUSINESS

PAPERS AND DISCUSSION FROM THE 1996 UNIVERSITY OF ARIZONA/FINOVA FORUM

Sponsored by The Finova Group, Inc.,
The College of Business and Public Administration

University of Arizona, Tucson, Arizona

February 29-March 2, 1996

ADVANCES IN
THE STUDY OF ENTREPRENEURSHIP,
INNOVATION, AND ECONOMIC GROWTH

THE INNOVATIVE MIDDLE:
POLITICAL AND ECONOMIC FACTORS
AFFECTING MID-SIZE BUSINESS

Editor: GARY D. LIBECAP
Director, Karl Eller Center
University of Arizona

VOLUME 8 • 1996

 JAI PRESS INC.

Greenwich, Connecticut   *London, England*

CONTENTS

INTRODUCTION:
THE ENTREPRENEURIAL MIDDLE

Gary D. Libecap

It was Sam Eichenfield's insight that mid-size business, one of the most dynamic and entrepreneurial sectors of the American economy, was overlooked in policy discussions and in the press. Sam Eichenfield is Chairman and CEO of The FINOVA Group Inc., a NYSE-listed company, that provides financial services to mid-size businesses. Through the Small Business Administration and Chamber of Commerce, small businesses have effective advocates at the federal, state, and local government level. Data are collected and analyzed by academic researchers on the role played by small business in the economy. Similarly, through the Conference Board and other institutions, large corporations receive attention and exert influence on policy. Mid-size businesses, companies with sales revenues from $10 to $300 million, heretofore have not been well represented. This condition largely is due to the heterogeneity of the group—it cuts across all industry sectors so that there has been no obvious bond across firms. The problems faced by firms in retail, textiles, communications, resorts, transportation, finance, and medical care, can vary sharply, making a uniform position on reform difficult. Yet, the importance of mid-size business in the growth of the American economy is so important that it cannot be overlooked. Research must be focused on its contributions and policies must be directed to its expansion.

Although the following data blend both small and mid-size business (itself an indication of the problem), they indicate the vitality and entrepreneurship associated with this sector. For example, from 1990 to 1994, more small and mid-size firms started than closed; whereas more large firms closed than opened. Small and mid-size businesses created more high-paying jobs than did their larger counterparts, and small and mid-sized businesses were leaders in the development and spread of vital, new technology. At this time of concern over corporate downsizing and lagging productivity growth, greater attention is warranted for this sector of the economy to promote entrepreneurship and expansion. With this objective in mind, the FINOVA GROUP and the University of Arizona have inaugurated The University of Arizona/FINOVA Forum to address the political and economic factors affecting mid-size business. The objectives are to draw the attention of researchers and policymakers to the contributions and concerns of mid-size business. Additionally, the forum will promote interaction among mid-size companies to discuss issues of common interest.

The first Forum was held February 29 through March 2, 1996, with the participation of more than three dozen executives of mid-size businesses. A list of the participants is provided at the end of this chapter. Four issues, ranging from regulatory and tort reform to government downsizing and changing tax laws, formed the structure of the Forum. Each topic was introduced by a policy expert, who presented a paper outlining the issues. Those and related papers, are presented in this volume.

I. REGULATION

In his paper, "The Overlooked Middle: Government Regulation and Mid-Size Business," Murray Weidenbaum, Director of the Center for the Study of American Business at Washington University, provides an overview of government regulation and its costs to American firms. Too often, Weidenbaum argues, cost-benefit analyzes are not done, so that a balanced view of the effects of regulation are missing. These costs are high, exceeding $500 billion annually. Regulations may be socially beneficial, but they must contribute at least what they cost society in order to promote growth in welfare. Regulation affects research and development, productivity, and capital formation. Other costs are: "(1) the cost to the taxpayer for supporting a galaxy of government regulators; (2) the cost to the consumer in the form of higher prices to cover the added expense of producing goods and services under government regulation; (3) the cost to the worker in the form of jobs eliminated by government regulation; and (4) the cost to society as a result of a reduced flow of new and better products and a less rapid rise in the standard of living."

According to Weidenbaum, the mid-size sector of American business is particularly affected because it is neglected in professional and public policy discussion. As a result it is penalized by regulatory legislation. Conversely, large firms are benefitted by their political influence and the availability of data which exists about their interests. Political pressures and equity concerns result in legislation that often exempts small businesses from many regulations and reduces their cost of compliance. Aptly named, mid-size companies are squeezed in the middle. Hence, existing regulatory legislation favors large companies and small firms. Mid-size companies have major disadvantages in coping with regulations. First, they cannot achieve the economies of scale realized by large organizations. Compliance expenditures are relatively more costly for mid-sized firms. As an example, at a time when companies with 2,000-5,000 employees reported costs of compliance with OSHA rules at $237 per employee, firms with 500-1,000 employees had average costs twice that level. Second, the lobbying efforts of national trade associations and others tend to reflect the interests of the largest member companies. Individually, mid-size companies find it too costly to maintain a permanent lobbying presence, especially at the federal level. Regulatory reform is unlikely to address the particular problems faced by middle market businesses. Third, mid-size firms typically face regulation by various authorities at all levels of government. Small businesses are less likely to be subject to the range of different regulations imposed by various government entities.

Murray Weidenbaum points out that the exemption enjoyed by small firms varies with different regulatory acts. As examples, companies with 14 or fewer employees are exempt from the Americans with Disabilities Act and from Title VII of the Civil Rights Act of 1964. Employers with 19 or fewer workers are exempt from the Age Discrimination and Employment Act. "There are a cluster of federal regulations that take effect when the company hires its fiftieth employee." He suggests that in some situations a growing company may elect to forego growth to avoid the costs of compliance with legislation that becomes effective with the 15th or 50th employee. Weidenbaum suggests substantial regulatory reform across the board, including:

- A requirement of benefit-cost analysis in each key stage of the regulatory process. This includes reviewing the operation of existing regulatory programs.
- When permits are required, a fixed time table should be specified.
- Legislation should emphasize objectives rather than precise methods to achieve objectives.
- Risk management should be an integral part in setting priorities.
- Legislation should promote regulatory justice. Costs should not be imposed on innocent parties, and compensation should be paid if regulation seriously reduces property rights.

II. LITIGATION REFORM

In Chapter 2, "Mid-size Businesses, Rule-making Theory, and Litigation Reform: Beware the Congressmen Bearing Gifts,"

Jonathan Macey, Director of the John M. Olin Program in Law
and Economics at the Cornell Law School, argues that mid-size
businesses are at a significant competitive disadvantage concerning
litigation when compared with both large and small firms.
According to Macey, mid-sized businesses cannot take advantage
of the economies of scale which accrue to the legal expenditures
of large companies, and cannot spend the sums required to
implement effective legal prevention programs. Further, small
businesses are not attractive legal targets.

To outline the argument, Macey presents a model of litigation
that explains why there is an incentive for plaintiffs to initiate
relatively meritless claims and an incentive by defendants to settle
the claims rather than incur costs to have them adjudicated without
merit. If the costs of litigation are borne more heavily by the
defendant, settlement may be cost effective. A settlement decision
is also conditioned by the approach adopted by a company in
managing litigation—reactive or preventive. "A reactive approach
is when the company merely reacts to litigation, and takes few steps
to prevent the initiation of lawsuits against itself. A preventive
approach is when the company takes affirmative steps to prevent
the initiation of litigation." Affirmative steps involve action "in
order to anticipate and prevent both litigation and regulatory
challenges. Generally, the preventive approach requires significant
up-front investment of both time and capital."

Macey concludes that mid-size companies pay a relatively
greater amount per dollar of sales for legal defense activities
compared with large companies. Based on the litigation model,
"a plaintiff with a marginal claim against a medium-size company
will more likely be met with a settlement offer—and therefore
success—than if the same marginal claim were made against a
larger company. It follows that a plaintiff has incentive to sue a
medium-size company on a marginal claim rather than a larger
company." Macey also maintains that mid-size companies find it
difficult to adopt a strategy of intense defensive litigation in order
to establish a reputation for not settling. He argues that it is
unlikely that any mid-size company could afford this strategy for
the length of time required to develop this reputation.

Macey also asserts that securities law penalizes mid-size companies. Relative to large firms, smaller ones experience greater stock price volatility. This volatility attracts class action lawsuits. Also, economies of scale are characteristic of legal activities. Defendant companies' costs include extensive discovery and expert witnesses, in addition to the possibility of adverse publicity and the cost of distracting company managers from their business concerns. This condition contrasts with the costs to plaintiffs which involve little or no discovery and where the principal costs are the time of lawyers in drafting complaints and negotiating settlements. Regarding securities and tort reform, Macey is pessimistic about the effect of reform on mid-size businesses. "Middle-size businesses are handicapped in their organizational efforts because they represent so many disparate interests. Too large to be considered small businesses and too small to be powerful lobbies as individuals, the middle really has only one unifying interest: resistance." He argues that large and small businesses obtain favors from the government in exchange for political support and these benefits are paid for by the rest of society.

Macey is more optimistic about reform at the local government level, where mid-size firms may have considerable political clout. For this reason, mid-size market companies have an interest in resisting efforts to federalize an issue such as tort reform. Accordingly, mid-size businesses must find common ground with one another. Marginal reforms are not likely to assist them; the middle market must work for fundamental reform.

III. FISCAL POLICIES

Chapter 3, Fiscal Policies and Mid-Size Business, by James Alm of the University of Colorado focuses on how businesses will be affected by fiscal policy changes; who gains and loses from such changes; and whether these effects are desirable. Alm discusses recent efforts to reduce the federal government deficit, examines specific tax proposals and makes basic tax reform suggestions. Alm believes, as do most economists, that deficits are harmful to current and future generations and that balancing the budget should be a primary concern of Congress and the President. He points out that the impact of a balanced budget on mid-size business is highly uncertain and that the most obvious benefit to mid-size business would be reductions in interest rates that might occur with the passage of a balanced budget.

Alm addresses the question "who pays the corporate income tax?" and suggests four possible candidates: the owners of the corporations, the recipients of capital income from any and all sources, the individuals who supply their resources to the corporation, or the consumers of corporate products. Alm points out that many economists believe the most likely bearers of the corporate tax burden, at least in the long run, are the many individuals who own capital. However, this conclusion is not universally held even among economists, let alone among those who run the corporations.

He explores the impact of reducing capital gains taxes. The taxation of capital gains has changed frequently over the last twenty years and the effects of these changes have been the subject of an intense and unresolved debate. There is strong evidence that changes in the tax treatment of capital gains have a major impact on the timing of short-term realization of capital gains. He notes that the advocates of reductions in the capital gains tax argue that the response of capital gains realizations to tax rate cuts is large and persistent. As a result, they argue further, the cuts will generate such a surge in realizations that tax revenues will actually increase, thereby paying for themselves. Other benefits include an increase in personal savings and investment and more risk-taking; the creation of more productive jobs; and a higher rate of economic growth. Alm believes that the jury is still out on the magnitude of the beneficial results from a reduction in the capital gains tax.

Alm favors fundamental reform of our tax structure as opposed to piecemeal changes in specific features of specific taxes. He notes that there is increasing interest in such an approach, due largely to increasingly negative attitudes toward federal income taxes. This negative attitude toward income taxes results in part from the widespread belief that many individuals and businesses do not pay their fair share of taxes. There also are strong objections to the complexity of the income tax and the resulting high compliance and collection costs.

There are essentially two main issues in the desires for tax reform. First, nearly all suggestions for tax reform call for an overall reduction in marginal tax rates, with the debate focusing on whether the rate structure should retain some of the progressivity, or whether a single, flat rate (imposed on all income above some level) should be chosen. The second issue focuses on what tax base should be chosen. Taxes can be imposed on essentially any of three tax bases: income, consumption, or wealth. Since 1913 the United States imposed the tax on income. However, today there is widespread and growing dissatisfaction with the income tax which is generating support for alternative bases of taxation.

The following three problems associated with the income tax are among the most significant for mid-size business according to Alm:

- *Complexity* and the resulting difficulties that businesses face in determining their taxes. Studies have suggested that *mid-size businesses face higher compliance costs than large firms* with costs estimated as high as $1,500 per employee.

  The complexity of the income tax has been increasing for several reasons. One reason is that we have decided as a nation that the tax system is a suitable mechanism for encouraging activities that are deemed desirable, as well as for discouraging activities that are unacceptable.

  Another major reason for increased complexity arises from frequent changes in the tax code. Since the Internal Revenue Act of 1954, there have been significant changes in the tax laws on over 30 occasions. These changes—indeed, even the discussion of possible changes—create uncertainty in the minds of taxpayers and increased compliance costs.
- *Distortions in business behavior.* The income tax affects the investment and labor choices of corporations. It creates incentives to finance investment with debt rather than equity. It leads firms to keep profits within the corporation rather than pay dividends to owners. It influences mergers and acquisitions of corporations. It affects corporate

decisions on inventory valuation and it changes corporate decisions on tax-deductible activities. Given the potential for enormous tax savings with the introduction of special tax provisions, there are also incentives for businesses to spend money to influence the legislative process. Even though there is much uncertainty regarding the magnitudes of corporate behavioral responses, there is little doubt that taxes matter in significant ways for corporate decisions.

- *Effect on savings and capital formation.* Alm suggests that this is perhaps the most serious problem with the existing income tax. Under the income tax, the income from corporate capital is taxed twice: once when the income is taxed at the corporate level, by the corporate income tax and again at the individual level, by the individual income tax when the income is paid out to individuals. Such double taxation clearly reduces the return to saving and investment. *The current income tax, in effect, penalizes savings and encourages consumption.* There is abundant evidence that the savings rate in the United States is relatively low and declining. Consequently, nearly all proposals for fundamental tax reform seek to replace the income tax with some form of consumption tax.

With regard to changing the income tax rate structure Alm makes a clear and simple statement. "Income taxes reduce the returns from working, saving and investing." A reduction in marginal tax rates correspondingly will increase these returns, leading to improved incentives to undertake these activities. In particular, a reduction in marginal tax rates on businesses will certainly lead them to invest more, to hire more workers, to produce more goods and services and to reduce tax avoidance activities. He warns, however, that it is in the area of the magnitude of these responses where there is enormous disagreement.

He believes that there is a hierarchy of behavioral responses to any changes in marginal tax rates. First, and the most clearly responsive behavioral change, is the timing of transactions (e.g., capital gains realizations, foreign and direct investment).

Second, is the purely financial and accounting response where the form of the transaction is altered. Last, and the weakest response, is changing decisions regarding working, saving and investing.

Of all the choices to be made in tax reform Alm believes that the most important choice is the tax base. He points out that virtually all the current major tax reform proposals propose to change the tax base from income to consumption. He favors the choice of consumption as a tax base because it removes investment, savings and capital income from the tax base and has lower administrative compliance costs.

Alm focuses on the flat tax to illustrate the effects of a consumption tax on mid-size business. While there is much disagreement regarding the magnitude of the compliance savings, there is little question that the compliance costs for mid-size business would decline.

With regard to savings and capital formation it is often claimed that a flat tax would give incentives for firms to base their decisions on the underlying and fundamental benefits and costs of their actions, rather than on the tax benefits and tax costs of the actions. There is little doubt that expensing of capital purchases would generate an immediate and possibly dramatic increase in investment, and this would increase the rate of economic growth. There would also be winners and losers from the surge in capital formation. Fast-growing, capital-intensive sectors would clearly gain because capital purchases would be deductible. However, it is equally clear that there would also be losers. Businesses that are highly leveraged would lose because interest on debt would not be deductible. Businesses with unused depreciation and depletion allowances would also lose.

Alm believes that the introduction of a flat tax offers the potential for significant benefits in the form of increased economic growth and reduced compliance costs. However, the magnitude of these benefits is highly uncertain because no nation has ever introduced a flat tax, so there is no historic experience upon which to base predictions. He is also concerned about the transition problems in moving from the existing income tax to a flat tax. These problems are formidable because both the existing income tax and the flat tax system would have to be maintained for some period of time. The costs of such parallel systems could be very high.

It is far from clear that the tax system can be systematically, predictably and efficiently manipulated to encourage or discourage the specific action of businesses of any size, despite the almost incessant efforts of government to do so. Consequently, Alm suggests a general rule for appropriate fiscal policy toward mid-size business. Taxes should be imposed at constant marginal tax rates on a broadly defined consumption tax base, with minimal use of special tax incentives.

He concludes that at this time it may be more prudent to achieve many of the goals of consumption taxation by moving to a consumption tax rather than by tinkering with the existing income tax, even though the choice of a consumption tax presents some difficult transition problems.

IV. GOVERNMENT BUDGET REFORM

In Chapter 4, An Analysis of the Potential Impacts of Federal Government Budgetary Restraints on Mid-Size Business Firms in the United States, James Smith of the University of North Carolina examines the budget of the United States in an historical context and points out that concerns about the debt of the federal government being "too high" or "out of control" have been with us since the beginning of our country. However, until the late 1940s we had an implied policy of balancing the budget annually except in periods of crises or war, and running surpluses in other periods. Since then budget policy has been more permissive with respect to deficits, using them frequently as an instrument of economic and social policy. The last time the United States ran a surplus was 1969 and Smith does not see another surplus before 2005, if then.

He notes that during the period of 1980-1996 we made five legislative attempts to reduce that rate of growth in government spending and they all have failed primarily because of inadequate measures for resolving different political agendas. The end result has been a national debt that has grown from $900 billion in 1980 to over $6 trillion in 1996.

The inability to rein in our federal spending has resulted in calls for a Balanced Budget Amendment to the Constitution and our current dead-lock over the 1996 federal budget. The federal government is currently running on continuing resolutions with only five of the 13 appropriation bills that make up the so-called discretionary part of the budget signed into law. This is a risky and ineffective way to manage the fiscal affairs of our nation.

Smith describes how important the various economic assumptions are in achieving the goal of a balanced budget, with the interest rate and inflation assumptions being the most dominant in determining the revenue and expenditure projections. He also points out that no matter which assumptions we choose, there is an extremely good chance that they will be wrong. He personally feels that there is a good chance that the Congressional Budget Office projections being used by the President and the Congress to forecast expenditures and revenues to the year 2002 will turn out to be wrong and on the pessimistic side, which would be good news for those seeking a balanced budget in 2002.

According to Smith, the basic problem with the budget rests in the area called *mandatory spending*. The key components of mandatory spending are Social Security, Medicare and Welfare. Currently, 64 percent of government spending is made up of mandatory spending plus interest. The current Republican balanced budget proposal has this part of the budget increasing to 72 percent and the Democrats have it increasing to 73 percent. The big question is "will voters accept such a much small share of the budget pie going to soldiers, justice, the environment and other discretionary spending?"

Since the 1960s the government budget has been taking a larger share of gross domestic product (GDP) and the mandatory programs have been taking a larger share of the larger budget. If Medicare, Medicaid and Social Security are not drastically changed the moment of truth will be reached in 2011 when baby boomers start turning 65 at the rate of one every 8 1/2 seconds and the costs of these programs explode.

Smith does believe that there will be absolute cuts in discretionary spending and a slowing of the growth of mandatory spending. He urges mid-size business to analyze carefully what

lines of business they are in and to search for government programs
that directly affect them so that they are prepared when the budget
adjustments finally come.

Smith concludes with an extensive list of the potential positive
economic results of a decline in government spending as a share
of GDP. They include: lower interest rates, higher saving and
greater investment, faster rates of growth of productivity, higher
employment, higher disposable income and higher corporate
profits. These outcomes will be very favorable for the economic
and business climate in the early twenty-first century. However,
for all these good things to happen, the Congress, the President
and the voters must be willing to make the hard choices now to
avoid a fiscal crisis in the first part of the twenty-first century.

V. FURTHER ISSUES OF TAX REFORM: A CONSUMPTION TAX

In Chapter 5, R. Glenn Hubbard of the Columbia University
Business School examines consumption taxes as part of tax reform.
Hubbard argues that current U.S. tax law distorts the allocation
of the nation's capital stock and reduces savings and investment.
This problem particularly affects entrepreneurial firms that seek
capital for expansion. He discusses some of the key problems in
the current tax system prompting calls for fundamental tax reform.
Hubbard then evaluates consumption taxes as an alternative to the
current tax system. In that evaluation, he notes that much of the
gains in economic efficiency, simplicity, and fairness accomplished
by moving from the current tax system to a broad-based
consumption tax could also be accomplished by reform of the
income tax. The Appendix to the chapter describes similarities and
differences among alternative consumption tax plans.

Current U.S. tax law treats corporations and their investors as
separate entities. Under this so-called "classical" system of
corporate taxation, two levels of tax are levied on earnings from
investments in corporate equity. First, income earned by
corporations is taxed at the corporate level. Second, when the
corporation distributes dividends to shareholders, the income is

taxed at the shareholder level as ordinary income. Undistributed earnings, which increase share values, are also double taxed, since they are taxed at capital gains rates when shares are sold. This practice, according to Hubbard, reduces incentives for investment.

There have been a variety of efforts to tax corporate income only once, called "integration" of the corporate and individual income taxes. These efforts are guided by the notion that fundamental economic considerations, not the tax structure, should guide investment, organizational, and financial decisions. Although the Tax Reform Act of 1986 reduced the effect of taxation on many business decisions, that reform did not directly address distortions in business organizational and financing decisions under current law. Thus, integration can be viewed as the next logical step in tax reform.

Hubbard argues that the current system of business income taxation raises questions of fairness because it creates differences in the taxation of alternative sources of income from capital. A taxpayer conducting an equity-financed business in corporate form faces a different tax burden than a taxpayer conducting the same business in noncorporate form. A corporation that raises capital in the form of equity faces a different tax burden than a corporation that raises the same amount of capital from debt. A similar disparity exists in the treatment of corporations that finance investment with retained earnings and those that pay dividends and finance investment with new equity. Because of its bias towards debt, the current tax system encourages taxpayers to engage in practices that tend to disguise equity as debt. This effort represents a wasteful use of resources, and imposes significant administrative costs in attempting to distinguish debt from equity. These arguments for integrating the corporate and individual income tax systems have been put forth by economists and legal specialists for more than a generation according to Hubbard.

The chapter turns to the issue of the "consumption tax" as a form of tax reform. The base of a broad-based consumption tax is households' consumption, not households' net income. "Consumption taxes" can be collected from businesses, households, or both. They can be familiar sales taxes, but do not have to be. Further, consumption taxes can incorporate exemptions and graduated marginal tax rates, as under the income tax. Many economists support the use of consumption taxes to replace the current individual and corporate income taxes. This support reflects efficiency, fairness, and simplicity concerns.

According to Hubbard, the nation would enjoy three sources of efficiency gains from moving to a broad-based consumption tax. First, the removal of the current tax on returns to new saving and investment increases capital accumulation and, ultimately, household incomes. Second, consumption taxation may stimulate business investment. Third, a broad-based consumption tax avoids potentially costly distortions of firms' financial and organizational structure. Taken together, efficiency gains from moving to a consumption tax are potentially dramatic. Additionally, with respect to fairness, consumption represents a better measure of "ability to pay" than does current income, because households' consumption decisions depend on wealth and expected future income as well as current income. Finally, a properly designed broad-based consumption tax promotes simplicity.

Hubbard describes how we might move from the current tax system to a broad-based consumption tax by considering the following three themes: (1) integrating the corporate and individual tax, (2) broadening the base and reducing marginal tax rates, and (3) moving to consumption taxation. Each of these processes is described in detail.

VI. THE FEDERAL RESERVE AND FINANCIAL POLICY: ANALYSIS FOR MID-SIZE BUSINESS

The final chapter by Donald Wells of the University of Arizona, "Forecasting U.S. Economic Trends for Use by Mid-Size Business: The Role of the Federal Reserve," provides suggestions on how financial data might be used by managers in planning. Wells argues that managers and owners of mid-size businesses will find it to their advantage to attempt forecasts of national economic activity. Trends in GDP, prices, employment, and interest rates constitute the backdrop for decisions of individual businesses with their own product mix and industry specific conditions, problems, and prospects. Economic forecasts are available in the general financial and economics press, but unless the reader has some basis for independent judgment, it is difficult to assess these forecasts, especially when there are substantial differences of opinion about the direction of the U.S. economy. The information required to make these judgments is readily available and does not require a major time commitment.

The limitations of the analysis should be recognized, however, according to Wells. It provides a forecast of broad trends in the economy but does not attempt any degree of precision. Professional forecasts are made to the tenth of a percentage point, but professional forecasts are revised frequently, typically each quarter. Is the owner of a business any better off with a forecast of GDP growth of 2.4 percent compared with one that expects an increase of GDP between 2 and 3 percent? For most, the latter probably will suffice.

Under conditions of substantial inflation or a major recession, the basic analysis will be less useful. Under these conditions the velocity of money becomes more unpredictable and influential. In these circumstances the impact on aggregate expenditures and GDP of changes in the monetary base and the money supply will be more difficult to predict. Finally, the analysis, like all forecasts, is not helpful in anticipating major shocks to the system such as regional conflicts, major financial upheavals, or disruptions to normal commerce such as the OPEC boycott of oil deliveries to the United States during the early 1970s. Nor can it predict the policy responses to these events in Washington, D.C.

Recognizing these limitations, Wells asks what forecast would a non-professional make about economic activity in 1996? The monetary base increased by 4.1 percent from June 1994 through December 1995. The comparable figures for M2 is 3.3 percent. For the last half of 1995, the monetary base increased by only 1.5 percent, while M2 increased by 5 percent. GDP growth in 1995 was less than 2 percent, and the rate of inflation as measured by the consumer price index ranged between 2.5 percent and 3 percent. The slow rate of growth of the monetary base in the last half of 1995 suggests that any increase in M2 during 1996 will be moderate. With anticipated steady but moderate growth in aggregate expenditures, it is reasonable to forecast a continuation of moderate increases in real GDP of between 2 and 3 percent and a rate of inflation of less than 3 percent. With the federal funds rate approximating 5.5 percent at the end of 1995, down slightly from nearly 5.75 percent earlier in the year, it appears that the availability of bank reserves is consistent with moderate increases in the federal funds rate, but in the absence of new inflationary pressures, interest rates in general should not increase substantially during 1996.

The basic structure of U.S. international payments and receipts in early 1996 remains the same; a current account deficit is counterbalanced by a surplus on capital account. Financial markets in the United States remain relatively strong, and that, plus the relative strength of the U.S. dollar in international markets, suggests foreign financial inflows into the United States will remain strong and will help in restraining interest rate increases. Throughout the chapter, Wells provides definitions and a general primer on how to interpret financial data.

All in all the papers in this volume provide important information for owners and managers of the entrepreneurial middle—mid-size business. There are a host of policy reforms under discussion, and these will importantly affect how this vital segment competes in the U.S. economy. Moreover, how these firms fare in policy change will determine how well the U.S. economy competes in the broader global economy.

APPENDIX

List of Participants at the UA/FINOVA Forum

Warner W. Abel, Jr., V.P., Finance and CFO, GLNX Corporation, The Woodland, TX

James Alm, Professor of Economics, University of Colorado, Boulder, CO

Terry Anderson, Political Economy Research Center, Bozeman, MT

Alex Aydin, Vice President, Procom Technology, Inc., Irvine CA
Larry S. Bird, Concord Hospitality, Inc., Lincoln, NE
Bill Bixel, Justice Finance Company, Dallas, TX
Robert Brown, Pegasus Capital Corporation, San Francisco, CA
Robert Burlingame, Burlingame Industries, Inc., Rialto, CA
Robert A. Byers, President, Tri-Anim Health Services, Inc., Sylmar, CA
Al Carter, President & CEO, Peppermint Music, Altanta, GA
Robert Crandall, The Brookings Institute, Washington, DC
Charles W. Gerber, Triumph Worldwide Companies, Ltd., New York, NY
Jody Gessow, The Argosy Group, Inc., Cypress Pointe Resorts, L.P., Woodside, CA
Ronald Gilson, Stanford Law School, Stanford University, Stanford, CA
Phillip Giordano, Calender Broadcasting Co., Middletown, NJ
Victor Goldberg, Columbia University Law School, New York, NY
Walter Greig, President, Enduro Systems, Inc., Houston, TX
J. Richard Hayes, Director, Financial Services, Brunswick Indoor Recreation Group, Lombard, IL
Roy E. Hayes, Jr., Bay Cable, Inc., Annapolis, MD
Constance Horner, The Brookings Institute, Washington, DC
Glenn Hubbard, Graduate School of Business, Columbia University, New York, NY
Tom Jacobs, Computer Town, Inc., Salem, NH
Morton Kamien, Kellogg School of Business, Northwestern University, Evanston, IL
Paul Katsenes, Deputy Director, City of Phoenix Community & Economic Development Agency, Phoenix, AZ
Simon Li, Micro Products Center, Huntingdon, PA
Milton Pierce, Western Shamrock, San Angelo, TX
Charles Plosser, Simon School of Business, University of Rocherster, Rochester, NY
James Rogers, Sunbelt Broadcasting Co., Las Vegas, NV
Selig D. Sacks Esq., Pryor, Cashman, Sherman & Flynn, New York, NY
Paul Savasta, Ingram Micro, Williamsville, NY

Glen Schnablegger, Reliant Finance, Anaheim, CA
Allen Shaw, President & CEO, Crescent Communications Corp., Winston-Salem, NC
Greg Skjonsby, CIG Financial, Irvine, CA
Tim Stripe, Winners Circle, Carlsbad, CA
Paul Tanner, Polyphase Corporation (IBM Foods), Dallas, TX
Howard Tecklin, President & CEO, Teckson Fabrics, Inc., New York, NY
Jim Thaxton, C.L. Thaxton & Sons, Lancaster, SC
Vito R. Vicenti, Law Offices of Vito R. Vincenti, New York, NY
William Weller, Crescent Communications Corportation, Greensboro, NC
Donald Wolk, Goodway Graphics, Jenkintown, PA
Jeffrey Wurst, Attorney, Ruskin, Moscou, Evans, Mineola, NY
G. Douglas Young, Young Warnick Cunningham & Co., Phoenix, AZ

THE OVERLOOKED MIDDLE:
GOVERNMENT REGULATION AND
MID-SIZE BUSINESS

Murray Weidenbaum

The rapid growth of government regulation of business in the United States has generated widespread concern over its costs and impacts. However, virtually all the attention has focused on either very large enterprises or very small businesses. A very substantial data base is readily available to the researcher in the case of the larger companies. As a result, most of the professional writing on regulation examines the subject from the viewpoint of the large enterprise.

Simultaneously, every public opinion poll on major institutions shows that Americans are suspicious of business, but love small companies. As a result, a combination of political pressures and equity

Advances in the Study of Entrepreneurship, Innovation, and Economic Growth,
Volume 8, pages 1-28.
Copyright © 1996 by JAI Press Inc.
ISBN: 0-7623-0185-6

concerns has resulted in numerous legislative provisions that
exempt small firms from regulatory requirements or reduce their
burden of compliance.

Because of these two developments, a very substantial middle
sector of American business is neglected in professional as well
as public policy discussions of regulatory matters. Let us try to
remedy this shortcoming. This report examines government
regulation from the viewpoint of the entire array of American
companies, but with special attention to what is the "overlooked
middle" sector. Medium-sized firms benefit relatively little from
the economies of scale generated by larger units or from the
legislative protections provided to smaller enterprises.

This chapter contains three sections: (1) an overview of
government regulation, (2) a focus on environmental regulation,
the largest and fastest growing portion of regulation, and (3) an
examination of public policies that benefit particular sizes of
business firms. Findings and recommendations are presented with
a view to reducing the costs and burdens imposed by government
regulation and simultaneously to introduce a greater emphasis on
fairness in treating different sizes of firms.

I. AN OVERVIEW OF GOVERNMENT REGULATION

No regulatory agency has a mission to depress the economy or to
raise the unemployment rate. However, many of their actions have
those undesirable effects. The barriers to economic growth imposed
by regulatory agencies are numerous and growing. Regulatory costs
are a hidden tax reducing the competitiveness of American business
and the availability of employment in the United States.

A.   The Many Costs of Government Regulation[1]

The popular view of regulation is wrong. It is not a contest
between the "good guys" (government and the consumer) and the
"bad guys" (business). The reality is that the consumer is at the
receiving end of the benefits as well as the costs generated by
government regulation. Business is the middleman (or woman).

The importance of regulation becomes apparent when the reader looks at the subject from the viewpoint of the average company. For each box on its organizational chart, there are one or more government agencies that are counterparts to that box: Environmental Protection Agency (EPA) and construction of new facilities, Occupational Safety and Health Administration (OSHA) and the workplace, Equal Employment Opportunity Commission (EEOC) and human resource policies, and so forth. Each of those alphabet soup agencies—as well as CPSC, FDA, FERC, FTC, FCC, SEC, ITC, NRC, IRS—is heavily involved in the company's internal decision making.

The impact of all these governmental rule makers is in one predictable direction: to increase the firm's overhead and operating costs, and to reduce the resources available to perform its major task of producing goods and services for the consumer. Government regulation results in the higher prices that consumers pay to cover the cost of compliance. But that domino effect makes regulation especially attractive to government officials. The costs do not show up in the government's budget (and thus do not have to be paid for by taxation). But citizens-consumers do not escape paying those costs—in the form of higher prices.

The EPA says that the cost of complying with environmental regulations came to $130 billion in 1994. That is not a static figure. Recently enacted legislation will add new costs in terms of billions of dollars a year. When researchers add in the costs of meeting the rules promulgated by several dozen other regulatory agencies—ranging from the Food and Drug Administration (FDA) to the National Highway Traffic Safety Administration— they come up with an aggregate hidden tax of regulatory costs of $500 billion a year or more (Hopkins, 1992, p. 5). If Congress had to appropriate another $500 billion a year to cover those costs, they would not approve so much regulation.

Going beyond the dollar signs, more subtle and far more serious burdens result from the tremendous amount of regulations that are promulgated. Central among these are the adverse effects on research and development, productivity, and capital formation. According to Professor Dale Jorgenson of Harvard University, by the time that the Clean Air Act is fully implemented in the year

2005, its impact (combined with that of previous environmental regulations) will reduce the nation's capital stock by 4.3 percent, increase the cost of capital by 5.5 percent, and reduce real gross national product by more than 3.0 percent annually (Costs, Benefits of U.S. Environmental Regulation, 1991). Those who think these are small numbers not worthy of much attention should consider how difficult it is to increase the rate of national output by 2 or 3 percent.

Regulation also reduces the flow of innovation and the production of new and better products because so many government regulatory agencies have the power, which they frequently exercise, to decide whether or not a new product will go on the market at all. For example, the major obstacles to the development of a new biotechnology industry are not financial or technological. They are regulatory.

The rising paperwork requirements of government agencies inevitably produce a lengthening regulatory lag. This delay often runs into years and is a costly drain on the time and budgets of private managers as well as public officials. In 1980, a California land developer obtained in 90 days what was then called zoning for a typical residential development. Currently, the typical company in that state receives an entitlement to build for one of its developments only after two years or more of intensive work.

In Mercer County, New Jersey, before work can commence on a new housing subdivision, the project must clear eleven separate reviews from nine different agencies, including seven on storm drainage. As the state's director of housing and development notes sardonically, even "jet fighter planes and moon rockets get by with triple redundant control systems." Developers estimate that, in New Jersey, government regulations add as much as 25 to 35 percent to the cost of every house they build.

Some of the housing regulations are just silly. An obscure 1992 federal law prohibits home builders from installing toilets that hold more than 1.6 gallons of water. The idea was to help conserve water. In practice, it often takes two or even three flushes to do the job. We have to wonder why the federal government has to become involved in such nonsense! (Staggenborg, 1995, August.)

Opening up new production facilities involves surmounting an even greater array of regulatory obstacles. William Ruckelshaus, former administrator of EPA, has described the process:

> Think of what it now takes to locate a new industrial facility. A company must obtain agreement from dozens of agencies at each of three levels of government, not to mention the courts. And it doesn't help to satisfy a majority of them. A single "no" anywhere along the line at any time in the process can halt years of planning, effort and investment.

Higher regulatory costs also have eroded the competitiveness of American companies struggling in an increasingly global marketplace. More stringent regulation of production in the United States quickly translates into fewer jobs and lower incomes to people in the United States. Moreover, American companies facing world competition are forced to seek lower cost locations overseas with more benign regulatory systems.

The justifications for the government's awesome regulatory power are numerous: federal rules promote a cleaner environment, a healthier work place, and keep unsafe products off the market. Unfortunately, the reality is often different. Consider drug regulation by the FDA.

Take the list of prescription drugs actually approved as safe and effective. In case after case, the United States was one of the last countries to permit their introduction. During the period 1990-1994, 92 of the 150 new drugs and vaccines approved by the FDA were approved first in other countries, including products for kidney cancer, partial epileptic seizures, migraine headaches, and fungal infections in AIDS patients ("Three-fifths of Drugs Approved in U.S. from 1990-1994 were Approved in Other Nations First," 1995).

The costs arising from government regulation are numerous: (1) the cost to the taxpayer for supporting a galaxy of government regulators, (2) the cost to the consumer in the form of higher prices to cover the added expense of producing goods and services under government regulations, (3) the cost to the worker in the form of jobs eliminated by government regulation, and (4) the cost to society as a result of a reduced flow of new and better products and a less rapid rise in the standard of living.

The benefits of regulation should not be overlooked. To the extent that the society obtains cleaner air, cleaner water, healthier work places, and safer products, these benefits are real. Please note these words carefully. The mere presence of a government agency does not guarantee that its worthy objectives will be achieved.

For example, Armco Steel Corporation was required to install special scrubbing equipment at one of its plants in order to reduce the emission of visible iron oxide dust. The scrubber does succeed in capturing 21.2 pounds per hour of the pollutant. However, it is run by a 1,020-horsepower electric motor. In producing the power for that motor, the electric utility's plant spews out 23.0 pounds per hour of sulfur and nitrogen oxides and other gaseous pollutants. Thus, even though Armco is meeting government regulations on visible emissions, the air is actually 1.8 pounds per hour dirtier because of the government's regulatory requirement.

The serious question is whether the regulation produces benefits and whether they are worth the costs. Society's bottom line is not the impact of regulatory actions on the government or on the business system, but the effect on the consumer, and on the citizen. Despite the protestations of the activists, economists breathe the same air and drink the same water as other people. But economists also raise serious questions: Does a given regulation produce benefits? Is it worth the costs? Is there a better way?

B.   Historical Trend of Federal Regulation

The historical trend of regulatory activities can be measured by changes in the size of the total work force of the federal regulatory agencies (see Table 1). After rapid growth in the decade of the 1970s (a 74% rise from 1970 to 1980), the regulatory wave crested. A 16 percent decline in the staffing of these activities from 1980 to 1985 reflects the substantial cutbacks in the early years of President Ronald Reagan's administration. During the Bush presidency, employment at federal regulatory agencies started an upward trend that has continued into the Clinton administration. In 1994, the regulatory headcount was an all-time high of 128,566; the fiscal 1996 budget projected a new high of 131,919.

Table 1. Staffing Summary for the Federal Regulatory Agencies (Fiscal Years, Full-time Equivalent Employment)

	1970	1975	1980	1985	1990	1994	(Estimated) 1995	1996	% Change 1995-1996
Social Regulation									
Consumer Safety and Health	41,463	51,237	55,213	45,056	50,243	58,194	58,150	58,392	0.4%
Job Safety and Other Working Conditions	6,486	12,334	17,894	14,229	13,610	12,817	13,012	13,565	4.2%
Environment	4,525	11,907	16,993	16,054	20,057	22,817	24,306	24,233	-0.3%
Energy	219	5,045	5,433	3,954	3,441	3,481	3,411	3,374	-0.1%
Total Social Regulation	52,693	80,523	95,533	79,293	87,351	97,309	98,879	99,564	0.7%
Economic Regulation									
Finance and Banking	4,969	6,401	9,524	8,864	13,049	15,544	15,441	15,368	-0.5%
Industry-Specific Regulation	5,675	7,013	7,483	5,296	4,629	4,615	4,912	4,980	1.4%
General Business	6,609	8,306	9,251	8,739	9,611	11,098	11,697	12,007	2.6%
Total Economic Regulation	17,253	21,720	26,258	22,899	27,289	31,257	32,050	32,355	1.0%
GRAND TOTAL	69,946	102,243	121,791	102,192	114,640	128,566	130,929	131,919	0.8%
Percentage Change		46.2%	19.1%	-16.1%	12.2%	12.1%	1.8%	0.8%	

Source: Center for the Study of American Business, Washington University. Derived from the Budget of the United States Government and related documents, various fiscal years.

7

The growth in regulatory staffing is reflected in the budgets of the federal regulatory apparatus (see Table 2). After reaching $8.8 billion (in constant 1987 dollars) in the last year of the Carter administration, these costs were decreased in President Reagan's first term. Federal regulatory budgets then rose slowly during his second term in office. President George Bush stepped up spending on regulation and President Bill Clinton has continued this trend. Nearly $12 billion (in constant 1987 dollars) were spent in 1994 to fund U.S. regulatory agencies. A further increase to $12.4 billion is budgeted for 1996.

The cost of regulation only begins with funding and staffing federal agencies. In several early efforts to quantify the larger impacts, the Center for the Study of American Business estimated the cost of complying with federal regulations at $63 billion in 1976 and $103 billion in 1979. Later research reveals that these costs are continuing to increase rapidly. In 1990, Rochester Institute of Technology economist Thomas Hopkins estimated the overall annual cost of federal regulation at roughly $400 billion, an average of $4,000 per household (Weidenbaum & DeFina, 1977; Weidenbaum, 1980, p. 23; Hopkins, 1992).

There is no evidence to suggest that the costs of complying with regulation have declined since 1990—or even stabilized. A recent report from the Business Roundtable estimates that the nation's regulatory system cost American businesses and citizens $581 billion in 1993. Without reform, this yearly burden is projected to reach $662 billion by the year 2000 ("CEOs Call for Sweeping Reform of U.S. Government Regulation," 1994).

C.   The Changing Nature of Regulation

Some background information is necessary in order to develop a constructive approach to regulatory reform. Until the 1960s, the industries subject to traditional economic regulation by government agencies—such as the Interstate Commerce Commission, the Civil Aeronautics Board, and the Federal Communications Commission—accounted for only one-tenth of the gross domestic product. Most sectors of the economy remained relatively unregulated, except for certain general standards of

Table 2. Summary of Administrative Costs of Federal Regulatory Activities (Fiscal Years, Millions of Dollars in "Obligations")

	1970	1975	1980	1985	1990	1994	(Estimated) 1995	1996	% Change 1995-1996
			Current Dollars						
Social Regulation									
Consumer Safety and Health	710	1,491	2,349	2,689	3,796	5,076	5,228	5,479	4.8%
Job Safety and Other Working Conditions	128	359	753	862	1,002	1,154	1,206	1,335	10.7%
Environment	214	841	1,651	2,495	4,164	5,232	5,360	5,920	10.4%
Energy	64	275	550	481	462	568	623	563	-9.6%
Total Social Regulation	1,116	2,966	5,303	6,527	9,424	12,030	12,417	13,297	7.1%
Economic Regulation									
Finance and Banking	86	151	362	624	1,080	1,290	1,429	1,384	-3.1%
Industry-Specific Regulation	91	160	279	289	320	454	473	497	5.1%
General Business	115	206	355	507	743	1,128	1,250	1,377	10.2%
Total Economic Regulation	292	517	996	1,420	2,143	2,872	3,152	3,258	3.4%
GRAND TOTAL	1,408	3,483	6,299	7,947	11,567	14,902	15,569	16,555	6.3%
Percentage Change		147.4%	80.8%	26.2%	45.6%	28.8%	4.5%	6.3%	

(continued)

Table 2. (Continued)

	1970	1975	1980	1985	1990	1994	(Estimated) 1995	1996	% Change 1995-1996
			Constant 1987 Dollars						
Social Regulation									
Consumer Safety and Health Job Safety and Other Working Conditions	2,017	3,030	3,276	2,849	3,353	4,022	4,031	4,104	1.8%
Environment	364	730	1050	913	885	914	930	1,000	7.5%
Energy	608	1,709	2,303	2,643	3,678	4,146	4,133	4,434	7.3%
	182	559	767	510	408	450	480	422	-12.2%
Total Social Regulation	3,170	6,028	7,396	6,914	8,325	9,532	9,574	9,960	4.0%
Economic Regulation									
Finance and Banking	244	307	505	661	954	1,022	1,102	1,037	-5.9%
Industry-Specific Regulation	259	325	389	306	283	360	365	372	2.1%
General Business	327	419	495	537	656	894	964	1,031	7.0%
Total Economic Regulation	830	1,051	1,389	1,504	1,893	2,276	2,430	2,440	0.4%
GRAND TOTAL	4,000	7,079	8,785	8,418	10,218	11,808	12,004	12,401	3.3%
Percentage Change		77.0%	24.1%	-4.2%	21.4%	15.6%	1.7%	3.3%	

Note: Numbers may not add to totals due to rounding.

Source: Center for the Study of American Business, Washington University. Derived from the Budget of the United States Government and related documents, various fiscal years.

business conduct, such as the antitrust laws and the exercise of state and local government "police powers" over public health. But that situation began to change fundamentally in the 1960s with the advent of social regulation, which now extends to virtually the entire American economy.

Although the traditional type of federal regulation of business continues, the regulatory efforts established by Congress in recent years follow a fundamentally different pattern. The new agencies (EPA, OSHA, EEOC) have broader jurisdiction than the traditional regulatory commissions (ICC, FCC, etc.). Yet, simultaneously, in important aspects they are far more restricted. This paradox lies at the heart of this new style of rule making.

The changing nature of regulation can be seen in Figure 1. The vertical lines show the traditional relationship between the old style of government commission and the specific industry that it regulates. However, most sectors of the economy—manufacturing, trade, and services—are virtually exempt from that type of intervention.

In contrast, the horizontal lines show the newer breed of regulatory agency. Their jurisdiction extends to the great bulk of the private sector. This makes it impractical for any single industry to dominate these regulatory activities. What specific industry is in a position to capture the EEOC or OSHA, or would have the incentive to do so?

Yet, in comparison with the older agencies, the new regulators in many ways operate in a far narrower sphere. They are not concerned with the totality of an industry but only with the one segment of operations that falls under their jurisdiction. The FCC, a traditional regulator, must pay attention to the basic mission of the television industry as part of its supervisory role. The EPA, on the other hand, is interested almost exclusively in the effect of those communications operations on the environment. This limitation prevents the newer agency from developing too close a concern with the overall well-being of any company or industry. But it also results in a lack of interest in the effects of its actions on a specific industry.

If there is any special interest that comes to dominate such an agency, it is not the industry being regulated but the group

12

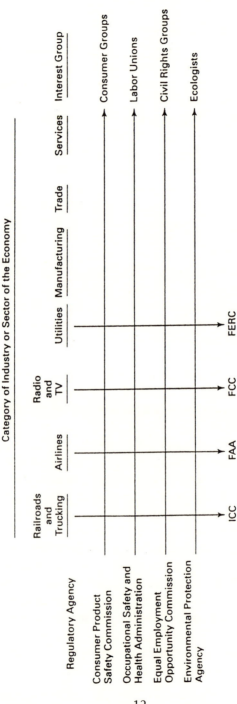

Figure 1. Patterns of Federal Regulation of Business

preoccupied with its specific task—ecologists in the case of environmental cleanup; civil rights, women's, and senior citizens' organizations in the case of elimination of job discrimination; labor unions in the establishment of safer working conditions; consumer groups in the reduction of product hazards; and so forth.

The results of the new approach in government regulation of business are the reverse of the traditional capture situation. Rather than being dominated by a given industry, the new type of regulatory activity is far more likely to utilize the resources of various industries, or to ignore their needs, in order to further the specific objectives of the regulatory agency and of its private-sector clientele.

II. ENVIRONMENTAL REGULATION

A 1994 survey of mid-size manufacturers in the United States reported that environmental regulations are the most burdensome regulations that they face. In answer to the question, "Which one area of government regulation would you describe as most burdensome?", 37 percent responded "environmental." In comparison, only 16 percent identified tax regulations, 15 percent workplace health and safety, and 4 percent product liability (*Fifth Annual Grant Thornton Survey of American Manufacturers*, 1994, p. 15; see also "Rating Regulations," 1995). Moreover, as noted in the previous section of this report, environmental protection is the most rapidly growing part of regulation. Thus, it is appropriate that this study give special attention to that aspect of government regulation of business.

As shown in the previous section, environmental protection programs are the most rapidly growing area of government regulation. This expansion has coincided with substantial progress in improving the quality of the environment. Yet the relationship between the cost of environmental programs and their benefits has not been as straightforward as would be expected. Frequently, citizens enthusiastically support environmental activities but are reluctant to pay for them directly, preferring business and/or government to cover the cost.

Environmental regulation covers a great variety of concerns—air pollution, water pollution, pesticides, toxic substances, hazardous wastes, unsafe drinking water, ocean dumping, noise emissions, and other adverse impacts on human health and ecological systems. EPA possesses an impressive arsenal of powers and duties.

A.   The Range of Environmental Regulation

The Clean Air Act of 1970 (including the amendments enacted in 1990) is the primary legislation dealing with air pollution. The complex regulations issued under it require four volumes in the Code of Federal Regulations. Attorneys specializing in this field have described this law as the environmental equivalent of the Internal Revenue Code—and that is not meant as a compliment (Anderson, Mandelker, & Tarlock, 1984). Among its many specific provisions, the Clean Air Act empowers EPA to establish national air quality standards.

EPA has established two sets of air quality standards for air pollutants, primary and secondary. Primary standards are designed to protect the health of the most sensitive group in the population. More stringent secondary standards are intended to clean the air of visible pollutants and prevent corrosion, crop damage, and any other effects of polluted air. Given the delay in achieving the primary standards, the secondary standards in practice have become something of a dead letter. EPA has established primary standards for six pollutants—sulfur oxides, total suspended particulates, carbon monoxide, photochemical oxidants, nitrogen oxides, and lead—and is authorized to establish standards for others.

After a year and a half of heated debate, Congress passed one of the most comprehensive environmental laws to date, the Clean Air Act Amendments of 1990. Among the provisions included in the statute's more than 700 pages are a phasing out of ozone depleting gases such as chlorofluorocarbons and carbon tetrachloride, as well as a significant reduction in sulfur dioxide and nitrogen oxide emissions. While innovative approaches such as performance-based standards and emissions trading provide

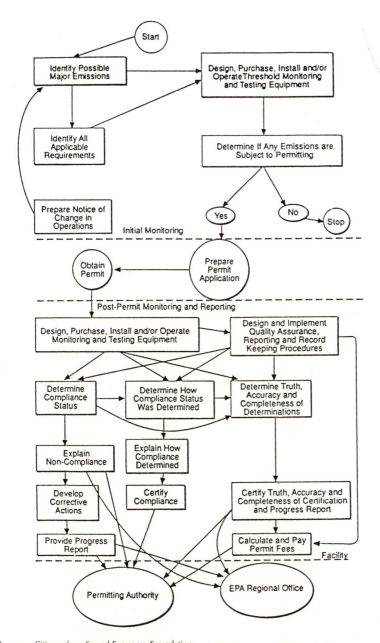

Source: Citizens for a Sound Economy Foundation

Figure 2. Company Compliance With the Clean Air Act

some flexibility in enforcement, the regulatory burden of the Clean Air Amendments ultimately affects every industry in the United States, from local dry cleaners to giant corporations. The sheer complexity of this legislation led a former director of the National Commission of Air Quality to declare, "No one is ever going to fully understand the impact of these amendments." (See Figure 2 for the array of business compliance activities.)

The Clean Water Act is the basis for the nation's water cleanup program. The act sets two specific national goals. The interim goal, commonly referred to as the "swimmable-fishable" goal, is to restore polluted waters, wherever attainable, to a quality that allows for the protection and propagation of fish, shellfish, and wildlife and for recreational use. The final goal—which in practice is more of a wish—is to eliminate all discharges of pollutants into the nation's navigable waters. Two very different basic control strategies are employed: (1) tough compulsory controls at the point of discharge for municipal and industrial polluters and (2) largely voluntary efforts for other sources of water pollution, such as runoffs from city streets and farms. Not too surprisingly, some of the major pollution sources are the non-point discharges from streets and rural areas (Lis & Chilton, 1992).

Specific provisions of the Clean Water Act have strong teeth. EPA can enter and inspect any polluting facility to check its records and monitoring equipment and to test its discharges. Failure to report the discharge of oil or other hazardous substances into the water can result in large fines. Dumping hazardous substances from a vessel can be punished with a fine of up to $5 million; also, heavy cleanup costs can be assessed to the polluter. Both the Clean Air and Clean Water laws empower citizens to bring suit against anyone violating these statutes.

Four major environmental statutes cover hazardous and toxic substances. The Toxic Substances Control Act (TSCA) gives EPA substantial power over the chemical industry, including the authority to require testing of new and existing chemical compounds and to require premanufacturing notices prior to the production of any new chemical or significant new use of an existing chemical. Under TSCA, EPA can control the manufacturing, processing, distribution, use, and disposal of any chemical substance and to require reporting of each chemical produced by every chemical manufacturer.

Under the Resource Conservation and Recovery Act, EPA regulates the disposal of hazardous wastes. Generators of wastes must create a record-keeping system to track the material from the point of generation to ultimate disposal. Under the Federal Insecticide, Fungicide, and Rodenticide Act, products to eliminate agricultural pests and diseases are controlled to keep hazardous chemicals off the market and to prevent "unreasonable" adverse effects on humans or on the environment. Manufacturers of new products must register with the agency.

The establishment in 1980 of a "superfund" to finance the cleanup of abandoned or inactive hazardous waste dump sites capped a decade of profound change in the environmental rules facing American business. In its first twelve years, the Comprehensive Environmental Response, Compensation, and Liability Act (the statute establishing the superfund) resulted in the collection of $12 billion, mainly from a fee levied on the feedstocks for the chemical and oil industries. Important changes were made by Congress when it renewed the superfund statute in 1986, especially in terms of increasing the funds available for cleanups. Through fiscal year 1992, EPA committed a total of $10.6 billion for cleanup projects.

One part of the new law, known as the Emergency Planning and Community Right-to-Know Act, requires nearly every facility that produces or uses any of 329 designated hazardous substances to make two sets of reports. First it must file detailed inventories of those hazardous substances with the local fire department. Secondly, it must report to EPA and designated state officials on the emissions of designated substances into the air, land, water, and waste treatment facilities—the toxic release inventory or TRI report. Thousands of companies are affected by the new reporting requirements, ranging from major chemical manufacturing facilities to local dry-cleaning establishments.

The new data requirements have generated some unexpected reactions, favorable and unfavorable. Few government agencies are geared to receive the vast quantity of information that is forthcoming. The comment by the chief of the Fire Protection

District of Valley Park, Missouri, is typical: "Some companies have already sent us boxes and boxes of this stuff. We don't have any facility to store it. If there was an emergency at a plant, by the time we went through all the information, it'd be over with" ("Chemicals," 1987).

The public focus on pollution by business firms results from a strange omission in the Community Right-to-Know provisions: government installations are exempt from the reporting requirements, even though some of the worst polluters are federal agencies such as the Departments of Defense and Energy.

B.   The Costs of Environmental Regulation

The costs of complying with environmental regulations are very substantial. For a great many American companies, a considerable portion of the funds available for modernization and expansion must be diverted to meet the EPA standards—or state environmental agency requirements. It has been estimated, that for each $1 increase in environmental compliance costs, total factor productivity is reduced by $3 to $4 (Gray & Shadbegian, 1993). That is a large loss of efficiency and competitiveness.

By increasing investment and operating costs, many environmental regulations work like a tax on capital equipment. This reduces total investment and capacity and thus leads to higher prices at lower levels of production. These high costs underscore the need to seek reforms of government regulation which can provide more cost-effective solutions.

III.   THE OVERLOOKED MIDDLE

As noted at the outset of this chapter, a great deal of regulatory legislation is so written as to lighten the burden on very small firms. However well motivated, such actions inevitably shift the focus of regulatory enforcement to other companies. This situation creates especial difficulty for the medium-size enterprises that cannot afford to maintain specialized staffs to deal with environmental, safety, workplace, and other complex regulatory requirements.

Table 3.   Mid-Sized Companies' Biggest Challenges

Category	Percent
Government regulation	52
Health insurance	20
Turning a profit	18
Taxes	18
Capital needs	14
Controlling expenses	9
Poor economy	5

Source: Arthur Andersen.

One modest-size company printing T-shirts recently bemoaned the fact that the Occupational Safety and Health Administration (OSHA) levied $2,250 in fines for such "serious" violations as using two-pronged plugs rather than three-pronged ones. The owner noted that if he had limited his payroll to ten people— his total labor force came to 14—he would have been spared this random inspection aimed at the giants of the printing industry (Doherty, 1994).

This adverse experience with government regulation is hardly unique. A recent survey by the accounting firm of Arthur Andersen reported that, by far, the biggest challenge facing mid-sized firms was government regulation (Merline, 1994) Over half of the companies listed regulations as the primary hurdle compared to only 18 percent who thought that "turning a profit" was the main problem (see Table 3).

A.   The Regulatory Burden on Middle-Size Companies

The presence of economies of scale in complying with government regulation is clear. The *Fortune* 500 fill out pretty much the same forms and meet the same requirements as smaller firms. The result is that the cost of complying with regulation is a higher percent of sales for the medium-size company than for larger enterprises. A survey of the cost of compliance with OSHA rules for different sizes of U.S. manufacturers showed very large variations. Companies with 2,000-5,000 employees reported an average cost of $237 per worker, while companies with 500-1,000 employees had an average cost of compliance of $467 per worker or almost twice as much (Weidenbaum, 1981, p. 195).

An earlier study of the legal costs to employers for a National Labor Relations Board election reported that companies with 100-149 employees experienced legal costs of $19 per employee eligible to vote, more than double the amount ($8) paid by companies with 1000 or more eligible workers (Imberman, 1975).

Professor Thomas Hopkins of the Rochester Institute of Technology has prepared estimates of the burdens of complying with federal regulation for different sizes of business (see Table 4). For companies with 20-499 employees, the regulatory burden per employee averages $5,298—78 percent higher than for companies with more than 500 employees. For very small companies (those with fewer than 20 workers), the unit compliance costs are slightly higher—4 percent, or well within the likely margin of error in these estimates.

B.   Exceptions for Small Business

Unfortunately, Congress has responded to the issue of uneven distribution of regulatory burdens in the predictable manner. It has not reduced the burden of regulation by streamlining the process. Rather, it has exempted different sizes of companies, based arbitrarily on the different regulatory statutes it was writing.

Table 4.   Federal Regulatory Costs by Size of Firm

Type of Regulation	Costs per Employee for Firms With		
	1-19 Employees	20-499 Employees	500+ Employees
Environmental	$1,246	$1,194	$671
Other social	658	630	354
Econ. efficiency	574	550	309
Econ. transfer	1,050	890	501
Process	2,017	1,931	1,086
All federal regs.	$5,532	$5,298	$2,979

Source: Hopkins (1995).

There is a host of regulatory exemptions for very small businesses. A facility with 9 or fewer full-time employees is not required to follow the procedures for Toxic Chemical Release Reporting Under the Emergency Planning and Community Right-to-Know Act. A company with a federal contract (or subcontract) of $25,000 or less does not have to comply with the Drug-Free Workplace Act. A contractor (or sub-contractor) receiving only a $10,000 federal contract, or a smaller amount, does not have to meet the requirements of the Rehabilitation Act ("Legal Reference Guide for Growing Businesses," 1995).

For all companies—even those not receiving a dime from the government—there is a bewildering array of size cutoffs, exempting some from one regulatory requirement or another. Companies with 14 or fewer employees are exempt from the Americans With Disabilities Act and from Title VII of the Civil Rights Act of 1964. Employers with 19 or fewer workers are exempt from the Age Discrimination in Employment Act and from the requirements of the Consolidated Omnibus Budget Reconciliation Act of 1985; the latter requires employers to provide certain health insurance benefits.

Firms with 99 or fewer employees are not covered by the Worker Adjustment and Retraining Notification Act. Companies with 99 or fewer participants in its employee benefit plan to not have to file a report each year with IRS by an independent qualified accountant.

There is a cluster of federal regulations that take effect when the company hires its fiftieth employee. These include the affirmative action program for companies working on government contracts, subcontracts, and grants and the Family and Medical Leave Act. The primary result is less dramatic than the issue of cost but far more fundamental. Yet it usually escapes public attention: the new reluctance on the part of some small businesses to expand. The result of the negative responses to the government's size cutoffs can be called the discouraged employer.

For example, WorldClass Process Inc., a new and growing Pittsburgh processor of flat-rolled steel coils, has increased its work force to 49. According to the company's chief financial officer, "We're going to keep at 49 as long as we can," in order to avoid being subject to the 50 or more employees threshold for coverage under the Family Leave Act (Bowers, 1993).

Similarly, the Schonstedt Instrument Company of Reston, Virginia, a profitable, high-tech firm, deliberately keeps its work force below 50 employees. It does so in order to avoid having to file Form EEO-1 every year. The company's president makes the point effectively, although not in scholarly fashion:

> ...a friend went over 50 employees on a government contract. He gave me his EEO file...it weighs more than 8 pounds...I have kept my employment under 50 (Schonstedt, 1992).

U.S.-based firms do not entirely escape this problem when they establish overseas operations. In Germany, companies with 10 or more employees must set up works councils, while in Belgium the cutoff is 50 and in France it is 100 (Johnson, 1995).

The most satisfying answer to this situation is not to raise the exemption ceiling now contained in many regulatory statutes in a misguided effort to assist medium-sized firms. Rather, public policy should reduce the proliferation and burden of regulation on all companies—and thus obviate the need for special exemptions to a lucky few. This important objective does not require dismantling the regulatory apparatus. It does mean developing more sensible and effective ways of responding to the public's genuine concern for a cleaner environment, a safer workplace, and other social concerns. That is the task of the following, and last, part of this report.

IV. ALTERNATIVE APPROACHES TO REGULATORY REFORM

What can be done to reform government regulation? The most satisfying answer is not to raise the exemption ceilings for a few more lucky companies, but to reexamine the fundamental basis for regulation. At the outset, the reader should be aware of the fact that the oldest government attitude toward business is to use command-and-control directives. In the Old Testament, the Book of Deuteronomy commands, "Thou shall not lend upon usury to thy brother." The ancient Babylonian Code of Hammurabi established uniform weights and measures and limited the rate of interest.

In contrast, most modern economists would rely primarily on competition in the marketplace to protect the consumer. Deregulation of interstate trucking, for example, is working. Since deregulation, thousands of new businesses have entered the trucking industry. The heightened degree of competition has forced sizable reductions in the cost of trucking which ultimately shows up in lower prices of all the items that move by truck.

This does not mean dismantling the entire regulatory apparatus. That is scare talk from the tenacious defenders of the status quo. It does mean developing better ways of responding to the public's genuine concern for a cleaner environment, a healthier work place, and safer products.

When government does regulate (as in the case of environmental pollution), economists prefer that government policymakers make the maximum use of economic incentives. After all, people do not pollute because they enjoy messing up the environment. They pollute because it often is cheaper or easier than not polluting. Thus, to an economist the environmental pollution problem is not the negative task of punishing wrongdoers. Rather, the challenge is a very positive one: to change people's incentives and habits.

The basic economic approach is that the price of a product should reflect its burden on the environment. If prices of goods and services were increased to reflect the costs imposed on the environment (perhaps as measured by cleanup costs), consumers would buy less of those environmentally damaging products. The idea is to get polluters to change their ways as high-polluting products become less attractive to consumers than low-polluting products.

A study of the Delaware estuary showed that effluent fees, set at a high enough level to achieve the desired level of water purity, would cost only one-half as much as a conventional regulatory program to achieve the same environmental cleanup.

What about the existing array of command-and-control regulation? Here, economists offer the notion of benefit/cost analysis to make sure that any given regulation does more good than harm. Benefit/cost analysis has been used for decades in examining government spending programs. It is neither a revolutionary, new idea nor an invention of the far right. In fact, such analyses have been attacked by both ends of the political spectrum. The far left does not like using economic analysis because not every proposal for government intervention passes a benefit/cost test. The far right does not like it either, because benefit/cost analysis can be used to justify government intervention.

Benefit/cost tests compensate for the fact that government decision makers on regulation do not face economic constraints. If the costs to society of a governmental agency action exceed the benefits, that situation does not have an adverse impact on the agency. The administrators may not even know about it.

Under the traditional approach they can crow about the benefits and ignore the costs—because the costs are transmitted to the consumer not by the government but by business. In fact, regulatory activists can enjoy needling business about price increases, even when they result from the costs of complying with the very regulations that the activists had urged be adopted. To an economist, "overregulation" is not an emotional term. It is merely shorthand for governmental rules for which the costs to the public are greater than the benefits.

In cases where dollars are an inappropriate measure of the impact of government regulation, there still may be opportunity for analysis in the decision-making process. For example, the drug that cures Rocky Mountain spotted fever also causes fatal anemia in one out of every 10,000 people who use it. A simple-minded approach would prohibit the use of this "dangerous" drug. Yet, the fever itself kills about eight out of every ten people who contract the disease. Thus, the benefits of the drug greatly outweighs the costs—measured, not in dollar terms, but in human lives.

Critics who are offended by the notion of subjecting regulation to a benefit/cost test unwittingly expose the weakness of their position. They must fear that their pet rules would flunk the test.

After all, showing that a regulatory activity generates an excess of benefits is a strong justification for continuing it. The painful knowledge that resources available to safeguard human lives are limited causes economists to become concerned when they see wasteful use of those resources because of regulation.

A.   A Comprehensive Approach is Needed

With hundreds of regulatory statutes on the books, it is not feasible for Congress to review and revise each of them. Instead, they should write one new law which will reform regulation across-the-board. Five key provisions would be especially helpful: (see Weidenbaum & Warren, 1995).

1. *A requirement for benefit-cost analysis in each key stage of the regulatory process–from writing the statutes to issuing regulations and reviewing the operation of regulatory programs.* Congress and the regulatory agencies should avoid an "at-any-cost" approach to achieving regulatory goals.

2. *When a statute requires citizens or organizations to obtain a permit, a fixed timetable should force the agency to act in a timely fashion.* If the agency is not able to process an application by the deadline, the permit should be granted automatically. The private sector should not be punished for the shortcomings of the public sector.

3. *Legislation establishing regulations should emphasize objectives sought rather than precise methods to be used for each regulatory program.* Detailed laws that place "legislative handcuffs" on agency administrators prevent more cost-effective solutions. On the other hand, legislators should avoid writing laws so vague that they know in advance that the courts will have to wrestle with the details. Congress should also refrain from passing regulatory laws with requirements that they know are not reasonably attainable. The notion of writing laws that are "technology-forcing" is wasteful of economic resources and encourages fruitless litigation.

4. *The federal government should use risk assessment to help set priorities for achieving greater protection of health, safety and the environment in the most cost-effective manner.* All risks are not equally serious. Government should focus on the most serious hazards. Sound science and comparative risk analysis should be drawn upon during the legislative drafting process. Regulating trivia harms the society by diverting resources away from more productive use.

5. *Congress should promote true regulatory justice.* Legislators and regulators should avoid imposing costs on innocent parties. Where regulation substantially reduces property rights, compensation should be paid. Finally, Congress should not retroactively apply laws to people for actions that were perfectly legal at the time they were made.

V. CONCLUSION

Now is an especially propitious time for Congress to embark upon significant reform and reduction of regulation. Such action would both respond to the widespread citizen dissatisfaction with and improve the lot of the overlooked middle-size company.

Government decision makers neglect an important fact when they adopt new or expanded regulatory requirements: government intervention often does more harm than good. Policymakers should not ignore the tremendous ability of individuals and private organizations to deal with the shortcomings that inevitably arise in a modern economy.

NOTE

1. This section draws on Weidenbaum (1995).

REFERENCES

Anderson, F.R., Mandelker, D.R., & Tarlock, A.D. (1984). *Environmental protection: Law and policy* (pp. 135-143). Boston, MA: Little, Brown & Company.

Bowers, B. (1993, October 15). Regulation play. *Wall Street Journal*, p. R16.

"CEOs call for sweeping reform of U.S. government regulation." (1994, June 21). *PR Newswire*.

"Chemicals." (1987, June 4). *St. Louis Post-Dispatch*, p. 12A.

Costs, benefits of U.S. environmental regulation. (1991, September-October) *Capital Formation*, pp. 1-2.

Doherty, P.R. (1994, September 21). OSHA makes certain you learn your lesson [Letter to the editor]. *Wall Street Journal*, p. A15.

Fifth annual Grant Thornton survey of american manufacturers. (1994). New York: Grant Thornton.

Gray, W.B., & Shadbegian, R.J. (1993). *Environmental regulation and manufacturing productivity growth.* Cambridge, MA: National Bureau of Economic Research.

Hopkins, T. (1995, November). *Profiles of regulatory costs.* A report to the U.S. Small Business Administration.

Hopkins, T. (1992). *The costs of federal regulation* (p. 5). Washington, DC: National Chamber Foundation.

Imberman, I. (1975, Summer). How expensive is an NLRB election? *MSU Business Topics*, p. 14.

Johnson, M. (1995, July). What will new EU ruling cost? *Management Review*, p. 22.

Legal reference guide for growing businesses. (1995, May). *St. Louis Small Business Monthly*, pp. 18-19.

Lis, J., & Chilton, K. (1992). *Clean water–murky policy* (pp. 40-44). St. Louis, MO: Washington University, Center for the Study of American Business.

Merline, J. (1994, September 8). Regulations hit small, medium-sized firms hardest. *Investor's Business Daily*, p. 1.

"Rating regulations." (1995, May). *Challenges*, p. 3.

Staggenborg, R. (1995, August 28). Small businesses flushed with ideas on regulations. *St. Louis Business Journal*, p. 17A.

Schonstedt, E.O. (1992, February 16). 'Robber Reg' has backfired [Letter to the editor]. *Washington Times*, p. B5.

Three-fifths of drugs Approved in U.S. from 1990-1994 were approved in other nations first. (1995, August). *PRMA Facts*, p. 1.

Weidenbaum, M.L. (1995). Government regulation of business. *Business and government in the global marketplace* (Part II). Englewood Cliffs, NJ: Prentice-Hall.

Weidenbaum, M.L. (1981). *Business, government, and the public.* Englewood Cliffs, NJ: Prentice-Hall.

Weidenbaum, M. (1980). *The future of business regulation.* New York: Amacom.

Weidenbaum, M., & DeFina, R. (1977). *The rising cost of government regulation.* St. Louis, MO: Washington University, Center for the Study of American Business.

Weidenbaum, M., & Warren, M. (1995). *It's time to cut government regulations*. St. Louis, MO: Washington University, Center for the Study of American Business.

MID-SIZE BUSINESS, RULE-MAKING
THEORY, AND LITIGATION REFORM:
BEWARE CONGRESSMEN BEARING GIFTS

Jonathan R. Macey

INTRODUCTION

Laws, regulations, and litigation affect different businesses
differently. This Article examines the effects of securities laws, tort
reform, and the litigation explosion on mid-size businesses in the
United States. I argue that mid-size businesses are at a significant
competitive disadvantage vis-à-vis the small and large firms against
whom they must compete in the marketplace.

Mid-size companies are at a competitive disadvantage against
large firms because large firms enjoy *economies of scale* that make
it relatively less costly for large firms to deal with burdensome

Advances in the Study of Entrepreneurship, Innovation, and Economic Growth,
Volume 8, pages 29-55.
Copyright © 1996 by JAI Press Inc.
All rights of reproduction in any form reserved.
ISBN: 0-7623-0185-6

regulation and vexatious litigation than other firms. These economies of scale result from the fact that (1) making public offerings of securities,[1] (2) defending litigation, and (3) lobbying Congress all involve fixed costs that large firms can amortize over a broader sales base; they can minimize the effects of these costs. Mid-size business is at a disadvantage against small business because small business is better organized to compete in the market for political favors. Indeed, there are entire bureaucracies—like the Small Business Administration—that cater to the needs of small business. Moreover, small business has overcome the economies of scale problems facing mid-size business by using its political clout to gain specific exemptions from regulations that affect it adversely—such as exemptions from registration requirements under the securities laws.

Middle-size businesses cannot take advantage of the economies of scale that accrue to the legal expenditures of larger companies, and cannot spend the sums required to implement as effective legal prevention programs. Small businesses are not attractive legal targets and are exempt from many regulations. Recent securities litigation and tort reform efforts have generally not addressed systemic issues like these, but rather have made relatively minor changes within the existing system. Since the existing legal system favors large and small businesses, mid-size businesses cannot truly benefit from these reform efforts. The better focus, not only for middle-size businesses but for all of society, is the fundamental nature of our political-legal system and how to work reforms on it.

Section I of this chapter presents a model of litigation that clarifies the incentive to bring meritless lawsuits. Section II discusses the litigation cost disadvantage mid-size businesses have relative to large businesses. In Sections III and IV, I consider securities litigation and tort reform efforts and present a rationale for the rule-making process. Section V addresses possible actions mid-size businesses can take to affect our rule-making system.

I.   A MODEL OF LITIGATION

The classic model of litigation posits that plaintiffs bring lawsuits in order to seek compensation for losses suffered by them, where the proximate cause of the loss is attributable to the named defendant through statute or common law. In this simple model, the plaintiff uses traditional litigation tactics to prove the defendant's liability. Courts under this model would dismiss meritless claims and sanction plaintiffs for bringing frivolous claims. The defendant would use traditional litigation tactics to contest marginal claims or would settle cases where the claim is clearly meritorious in order to avoid the costs of traditional litigation in addition to damages.[2] This traditional model, however, fails to consider disparate transaction costs and is therefore not satisfactory.

The following model shows that the traditional litigation model does not work (Buffone, 1995). Assume X and Y are two parties to a suit; X sues Y for $100. Further assume that X has a 60 percent probability of success at trial. Accordingly, assume that Y has a 40 percent chance of winning. Assuming no ill will—or similar personal obstacles—between X and Y, and that both X and Y agree that X has a 60 percent probability of success, they will settle the case in order to avoid the expense and inconvenience of litigation. In this case, X and Y will agree to settle for $60. This amount is the result of multiplying the amount of the claim ($100) by the probability of plaintiff's success (.60).

If, however, X and Y cannot agree on the likelihood of X's success at trial, then a settlement is not necessarily the most likely outcome. For instance, assume that X believes he has a 70 percent probability of success at trial, and that Y believes X has only a 30 percent probability of success on the merits. The expected value of the case to X is $70 ($100 times .70), while X's expected value as perceived by Y is $30 ($100 times .30). X would expect to receive $70 in any settlement, while Y would be prepared to pay only $30. Each party would likely reject any settlement offer by the other party based on their perceived expected value of the case. Thus, the greater the difference between each party's perceived probability of success on the merits, and therefore the perceived expected value of the lawsuit to the plaintiff, the less likely the parties are to settle the case without trial.

Now consider the original hypothetical in the presence of transaction costs. Assume that both X and Y will have to each pay $20 more to litigate the lawsuit than to settle. Further assuming that both X and Y perceive X's probability of success on the merits as 60 percent, it is likely that a settlement will be reached. X places an expected value of $40 ($100 times .60 minus $20) on the lawsuit. However, the expected loss to Y will increase from $60 ($100 times .60) to $80 ($60 expected loss on the merits plus $20 litigation expenses). Both parties have an incentive to settle at $60, which is the same settlement amount this simple model predicts before inclusion of transaction costs, assuming that settlement before trial avoids these transaction costs. If the parties reach a settlement for $60, X makes $20 more than he would if the case were litigated, and Y loses $20 less than he would if the case were litigated. Similarly, the inclusion of transaction costs in the model does not change the preference for trial over settlement as the difference between each party's perception of the plaintiff's probability of success increases.

The predicted outcome—settlement or trial—does change when transaction costs are not incurred by X and Y equally. Assume that both X and Y perceive that X has a 60 percent probability of success onthe merits, but further assume that X (as plaintiff) will incur transaction costs of $10 if the case goes to trial and that Y will incur transaction costs of $30 if the case goes to trial. X's expected value of the case after litigation is $50 ($100 times .60 minus $10), while Y's expected value of a trial is a loss of $90 ($100 times .60 plus $30). In this hypothetical, both X and Y will readily settle at some amount greater than $50 and less than $90; both parties prefer such a settlement to a trial.

Unequal transaction costs dramatically affect the likelihood of either settlement or trial when the plaintiff's claim has a low probability of success at trial. Assume that both X and Y perceive that X has a 5 percent probability of success at trial, and that a trial will cost $10 for X and $30 for Y. X's expected value of the lawsuit is −$5 ($100 times .05 minus $10). Y's expected loss from the lawsuit is $35 ($100 times .05 plus $30). Thus, Y has incentive to settle the lawsuit for some amount greater than zero and less than $35. X has an incentive to bring a lawsuit, regardless of its merits, as long as he realizes that Y will will lose money in the litigation whether or not Y wins the case on the merits.

In addition, X has an incentive to become a "repeat player"—to bring meritless lawsuits repeatedly—while any mid-size defendant, because they must pay disproportionately for legal defense, does not have an incentive to develop a reputation for fighting meritless lawsuits.[3]

Unfortunately, in the presence of litigation transaction costs that are unequal and more costly for defendants, the defendant has an economic incentive to settle essentially meritless claims for positive value, in order to avoid the costs which accompany courts' rejections of the claims. Furthermore, and perhaps more importantly, plaintiffs with meritless claims have an incentive to bring those claims; while a claim may have a negative expected litigation value to a plaintiff, it has a positive settlement value.

II. EMPIRICAL MODELING OF LITIGATION ISSUES IN MID-SIZE COMPANIES

The preceding section demonstrated that, where the transaction costs of litigation are borne unequally by the parties to the lawsuit, there is not only an incentive for plaintiffs to bring relatively meritless claims, there is an incentive for the defendant to settle the claims rather than incur costs to have them adjudged without merit. However, that simple model of litigation does not address the question of whether, given this incentive structure, mid-size companies are disparately impacted. This section discusses empirical research which indicates that mid-size companies do, in fact, bear greater relative legal costs than large companies.

Any company, regardless of size, can approach the question of managing litigation from two perspectives: reactive or preventative (Pashigian, 1982). A reactive approach is when the company merely reacts to litigation, and takes few steps to prevent the initiation of lawsuits against itself. A preventative approach is when the company takes affirmative steps to prevent the initiation of litigation. Affirmative steps typically involve interaction between in-house counsel (or firm lawyers) and management, engineering, and other personnel to, for example, rearrange production methods, alter work methods and activities of employees, and redesign products in order to anticipate and prevent both litigation and regulatory challenges. Generally, the preventative approach requires significant up-front investment of both time and capital.

An empirical study has considered the relationships between the preventative approach and company size. This study considered three aspects of the relationship between companies and legal defense (Pashigian, 1982, p. 248). First, the study considered the relationship between a company's expenditures on corporate legal departments and expenditures on legal defense activities. Legal defense activities consist of sums expended to defend in litigation or before regulatory bodies. At issue is whether internal expenditures on legal departments reduce expenditures on legal defense activities. Second, the relationship between legal defense activities and company size was considered. This part of the analysis asked whether legal defense expenditures increase, and if so to what extent, with the size of the company.

As to the practice of preventative law, the study found that the existence of an internal corporate law department anticipates problems that arise from court rulings and new regulations or regulatory bodies. In addition, legal prevention operates to not only reduce the aggregate number of suits that are brought against the company (relative to its size), but also improve the effectiveness of legal defense once a suit is brought. Professor Pashigian states:

> The practice of preventive law appears to reduce the number of suits and improves the effectiveness of the legal defense once a suit is filed against the company (Pashigian, 1982, p. 268).

The second part of the study considered the relationship between company size and the amount spent by the company on legal defense activities. The expected outcome, informed by facile marketplace observations, might be that the amount spent by a company on legal defense activities should increase linearly with the size of the company. Specifically, "common wisdom" suggests that if the size of a company doubles, for example, then the amount spent on legal defense would also double.

Surprisingly, this is not the case; significant economies of scale exist. In fact, companies with sales of $300 million per year spend approximately *3.5* times more on legal defense activities as a proportion of legal costs per million dollars of sales than do companies with sales of $6 billion per year (Pashigian, 1982, p. 261). This means that "the smaller companies...rather than the larger companies...are subject to relatively more legal harass-ment" (Pashigian, 1982, p. 262). There are several possible explanations for this apparent economy of scale. First, the effectiveness of prevention activities may increase as the aggregate amount spent on prevention increases. The data implies that the marginal return on a dollar spent for legal prevention in considerably greater for companies with total yearly sales of $300-1250 million than for larger companies (Pashigian, 1982, p. 261). Second, larger companies may have less need for legal services, in that they may have greater leverage to prevent the onset of legal or regulatory circumstances that require legal defense expenditures.

Finally, the study concludes that "smaller companies...are at a cost disadvantage in legal costs incurred" (Pashigian, 1982, p. 268). This is particularly the case as to matters of regulatory compliance:

> [S]maller companies have been placed at an increasing cost disadvantage in their attempts to comply with...government regulatory programs. Extrapolating our results to still smaller companies may be inappropriate if smaller companies are either exempt from or subject to less stringent enforcement by the regulatory authorities. [T]hese observations suggest a nonlinear effect of regulation....Smaller companies could be least effected because of exemption or less stringent enforcement. Medium-size companies are most affected because they are subject to enforcement and yet are not large enough to exhaust the economies of scale associated with compliance activities. The larger companies are also subject to enforcement but they at least are able to take advantage of the economies of scale in compliance (Pashigian, 1982, p. 268).

Small businesses are exempt from numerous government regulations, from the securities law, and are less attractive litigation targets because they have fewer assets. Almost every government regulation which imposes costs on businesses has a threshold below which the regulation is not applicable. For example, the Americans With Disabilities Act is not applicable to companies with fourteen or fewer employees, and the Worker Adjustment and Retraining Act is not applicable to employers with ninety-nine or fewer employees (see, e.g., Weidenbaum, 1996).

The benefits to small businesses from special applicability of government regulation are legion. Under S.E.C. Rule 12g-1, businesses with $5 million or less in assets are exempt from the registration requirements of the Securities Exchange Act of 1934. Under Regulation A, non-reporting companies that issue $5 million or less in securities in a twelve-month period are exempt from the normal registration requirements and may use a far less costly "mini-registration" (see 17 C.F.R. § 230.251-.262, 1995; The SEC's Small Business Initiatives and Regulation A: New Life for an Old Exemption, 1993). Regulation D exempts from the Securities Act of 1933 registration requirements limited private offerings and offerings below $5 million (17 C.F.R. § 230.501-.508 1995). Companies with 100 or fewer employees have obtained special environmental dispensations, such as fee reductions and grace periods to correct violations (Mehta & Selz, 1995). Small businesses also benefit indirectly from government action. For example, more stringent regulatory scrutiny of bank lending to small businesses has prompted banks to lend money to small companies at two points below the prime rate (Selz, 1994).

The fundamental conclusion is that mid-size companies, to the extent they are not excluded from regulatory or statutory enforcement, must pay a disproportionately larger amount for regulatory compliance and for legal defense activities when compared to larger companies. When considered in light of the simple litigation model, these disproportionate litigation costs result in unequal litigation transaction costs. Accordingly, a plaintiff with a marginal claim against a medium-size company will more likely be met with a settlement offer—and therefore success—than if the same marginal claim were made against a larger company. It follows that a plaintiff has incentive to sue a medium-size company on a marginal claim rather than a larger company.

III. SECURITIES REGULATION AND LITIGATION REFORM

A.   Justification for Regulation

Historically, the publicly articulated justification for the securities laws was that market forces did not generate the accurate information that investors and other market participants need to make informed decisions about how to allocate capital. The Securities Act of 1933 (15 U.S.C. § 77, 1988) prohibits offers and sales of securities which are not registered with the Securities and Exchange Commission (SEC), and prohibits fraudulent or deceptive practices in any offer or sale of securities. The Securities Exchange Act of 1934 (15 U.S.C. §§ 78a-7811, 1988, Supp. 1993) extends federal regulation to securities which are already issued and traded, and imposes disclosure requirements on publicly-held corporations. Congressional rationale for these regulations was that:

> disclosure in the glaring light of publicity would provide investors with sufficient information to be able to make informed investment decisions....[Securities regulation] had two basic purposes: to provide investors with sufficient material information to enable informed investment decisions and to prohibit fraud in connection with the sale of securities (Phillips & Zecher, 1981).

The rationale for securities regulation has remained unchanged. A former SEC Commissioner recently wrote:

> I know that effective regulation plays a vital role in maintaining the health and integrity of the financial markets. Investors must be confident that they will be fairly treated before placing their hard-earned savings at risk. Underpinning that confidence is an essential system of disclosure, oversight, and enforcement (Beese, 1995).

While these justifications sound appealing, advocates leave unstated that regulation also provides organized interest groups the opportunity to shape regulation into the form most beneficial to them—or harmful to their competitors—and that it provides politicians and bureaucratic personnel with wealth transfer opportunities and job security. Regulations also impose fixed costs on businesses that issue securities. Larger companies, therefore, find it less costly to comply with the securities regulations because they can distribute the cost over a significantly larger number of issued shares and over a larger sales base. While it is almost certainly true that securities regulation will be a fact of life for the foreseeable future, this does not imply that securities regulations and the costs they disproportionately impose can be rationally justified today.

Three closely related economic developments have greatly diminished market demand for the SEC and its fundamental regulatory philosophy (Macey, 1994). First, as financial markets have developed, they have become more efficient; the current price of a security in the market will be the best estimate of the future price, because the current price will fully reflect all available information about the future cash flows to the investors who own the security (Fama, 1970). Second, while the SEC has been forcing information into the marketplace for over six decades, uninformed traders still participate in the securities markets. However, the mere existence of uninformed traders does not justify regulation, because these uninformed traders *choose* to remain uninformed.[4] Furthermore, there is little need for regulations that force disclosure because the securities markets *require* information; corporations which do not disclose, or disclose untruthfully, will suffer considerably at the hands of market specialists. Finally, modern portfolio theory and capital asset pricing models provide investors with tools to understand and reduce risk that are far superior to regulatory methodologies (see, e.g., Markowitz, 1952; Sharpe, 1964).

B.   Securities Litigation: Need for Reform

To faciliate enforcement of the 1933 and 1934 Acts, Congress specifically provided that, in certain of the express liability provisions of both acts, any person found liable for regulatory violations would be liable for the full amount of the damages, regardless of the actual damages they caused.[5] Securities actions were also facilitated by the recognition of an implied private right of action-private individuals may sue to enforce the securities laws instead of the government—under the general antifraud provision in SEC Rule 10b-5.[6] Subsequent acceptance of the "fraud on the market" theory, which creates a presumption in Rule 10b-5 litigation of reliance on the public statements of a security issuer when the individual purchased the securities on an open and developed market, further encouraged securities litigation.[7]

Advocates of reform argue that changes in the system are necessary because of the large amount of money at stake in class actions, the growing number of securities suits, and particularly the unwarranted increase in the size of settlements recovered by plaintiffs and their lawyers (Junewicz & Hildebrand, 1995). Plaintiffs' lawyers contend that the number of securities class action lawsuits was approximately the same in 1974 as in 1994—about 300 per year (Lerarch, 1995, pp. 24-25). These same figures also reveal that there were 86 filings in 1981, about 100 per year through 1989, and a jump to 315 in 1990. Of greater concern is that securities class actions are generally filed within days, or sometimes hours, of a stock price decline or significant negative announcement (Policzer, 1992, pp. 1, 34). This indicates that very little pre-filing investigation is completed, and that perverse incentives dominate the class action regime.

High technology firms and smaller companies tend to suffer most from private enforcement actions under the securities laws, because their stock prices are more volatile.[8] Presumptions under private enforcement actions, such as the "fraud on the market" theory, place the burden of proof on the company charged with a violation, rather than on the plaintiff. Accordingly, the transaction costs of litigation to the plaintiff are generally low, involving little or no discovery and the cost of a lawyers' time in drafting a complaint and negotiating a settlement.[9] Conversely, defendant companies' costs include extensive discovery and expert witnesses, in addition to the possibility of adverse publicity and the cost of distracting company managers from their business concerns (see Boenninghausen, 1993, pp. 30-31). Because of this burden, all companies faced with securities litigation bear a disproportionate amount of the transaction costs in the litigation, relative to the plaintiff.

Based on the simple litigation model and empirical study discussed above, the disproportionate costs of litigation weigh more heavily on smaller companies. Not only are mid-size companies the target of more securities litigation as a result of greater stock price volatility, but the economies of scale operative in legal defense exacerbate their burden of litigation costs. Smaller companies are least able to take advantage of the economies of scale which are characteristic of large company legal activities. And since smaller companies have more volatile stock prices—representative of the attendant risks of smaller businesses—they have the most need for undiluted access to the equity markets because lenders will be unwilling to place their capital, in the aggregate, at such risk.

Because mid-size firms have fewer assets and should be less attractive securities litigation targets, plaintiffs have sought for defendants in securities suits who are better able to pay—"deep pockets" defendants—and have found them in accounting firms and other professional advisors. Joint and several liability features in the securities regulation have enabled plaintiffs to recover from these firms. Opponents of reform have argued that the number of suits against or involving accounting firms has not increased in recent years. However, the liability for the accounting firms is tremendous; the six largest accounting firms in the country presently face about $30 billion in liability claims under the securities regulations ("Witnesses Dispute Whether Reform Needed to Stem Spurious Litigation," 1993).

The effects of unleashing securities litigation upon "deep pocket" professional advisors have been dramatic. As the risk of excessive liability increases, professional advisors have reduced their risk exposure by avoiding initial public offerings and high-risk companies. The six largest accounting firms, subject to billions in liability, are increasingly declining audit engagements from middle-size companies, high-technology companies, and initial issue companies, all of which the accounting industry consider high risk (Arthur Andersen & Co. et al., 1992). Of mid-size accounting firms, 56 percent refuse to do business with high-risk firms (Arthur Andersen & Co. et al., 1992). Smaller firms are refusing to do audit work altogether, because audits generate only 6 percent of total revenues while resulting in 31 percent of total litigation costs (Burton, 1992). Of course, those accounting firms that still perform work which exposes them to liability in securities litigation must necessarily charge more for their services. The result is that mid-size companies not only must bear a disproportionate share of the costs of securities litigation, the cost to them of raising equity capital has increased beyond the direct costs imposed by regulation.

C. Shape of Securities Litigation Reform

This section will address only three changes recently made by Congress in the Private Securities Litigation Reform Act of 1995 (the Act).[10] These changes are relevant to joint and several liability, fee shifting, and pleading requirements.

Congress revised the traditional rule of joint and several liability—which held a defendant who was only 1 percent liable responsible for 100 percent of the damages—to a rule which provides that defendants who do not commit knowing violations generally will be liable only for the portion of the damages attributable to their percentage of responsibility. To commit a "knowing" violation, a defendant must make a material representation or omission with actual knowledge that it was false or misleading and that some person likely would rely on it (Hamilton, 1996, p. 28). Reckless conduct generally does not constitute a "knowing" violation.

Congressional "reform" will primarily affect the plaintiffs' lawyers choice of client, rather than deny them clients, because there are two significant exceptions that provide notable opportunities for plaintiffs' lawyers to evade the new rule. First, defendants are jointly and severally liable if the plaintiff is entitled to damages exceeding 10 percent of his net worth and the plaintiff's net worth is less than $200,000. This exception does not reflect a judgment that these plaintiffs are in need of special protection under the securities laws, but rather ensure that claims by the majority of investors would be unaffected by the change.[11] Second, if a defendant cannot pay its allocable share of damages due to insolvency, the other defendants must contribute an additional amount up to 50 percent of their own liability.

As to fee shifting, Congress did not follow a strict English rule— "loser pays"—regime. Instead, Congress strengthened the procedural requirements of Federal Rule of Civil Procedure 11 as to private securities litigation. Rule 11 ostensibly operates to enable federal courts to sanction lawyers for frivolous pleadings. Its application has, however, been a notorious failure; judges rarely apply sanctions and when they do the sanction is ineffectual (Hamilton, 1996, p. 30). The Act now requires judges to record specific findings of compliance with all Rule 11(b) requirements. If a party has failed to comply with Rule 11(b)—he has pleaded frivolously—the prevailing party is presumptively entitled to an award of his legal costs in the entire action, unless the Rule 11(b) violation is *de minimis*.

Federal Rule of Civil Procedure 9(b) requires that fraud—the general issue in securities litigation—be pled with "particularity." The Act strengthens this, again notoriously, weak requirement by defining "particularity." Under the Act, the plaintiff in securities litigation must specify each statement alleged to be misleading and the reasons why it is misleading. If the allegation is made based on information and belief, all information on which the belief is based must be set forth in the pleading. Facts which are claimed to have given rise to a "strong inference" must be specifically alleged. The Act also, generally, stays all discovery pending a ruling on a motion to dismiss.

D.   Likely Effect of Some Securities Litigation Reform

Two competing theories have been offered to explain the role of government in regulating society: the public-interest theory and the interest-group theory. Public-interest theory holds that regulation can solve collective action problems and push markets into a socially optimal equilibrium.[12]

The economic, or interest-group, theory of regulation asserts that legislation is a good demanded and supplied much as other goods. Politicians act to maximize their self-interest—election or reelection—by exchanging political support, campaign contributions, and similar currencies for legislation which benefits the discrete and organized distributional coalitions that desire such legislation. This is not to say that politics is corrupt or venal. Rather, democracy by its very nature places politicians in a Darwinian struggle for survival in the form of votes. The economic theory of regulation posits that legislation will benefit those interests that organize in order to provide the politician with necessary political support. The costs of providing benefits to these distributional coalitions will be paid for by those in a democracy who cannot or do not organize to protect their own interests.

Government regulation of any sphere of conduct allows individuals, organizations, and coalitions to exchange money for favorable legislation. The SEC, for example, is a powerful regulatory body; one of its fundamental interests is protecting its own regulatory "turf." The SEC's regulatory "turf" provides a basis to exchange favorable regulation for political capital[13] This behavior has prompted an observer of securities litigation reform efforts to comment that "This Congress has put the legislative process up for sale to the highest bidder" (Siconolfi & Raghaven, 1995). In such a lawmaking environment, it is almost specious to expect fundamental and genuine "reform." Such an effort is counter to the interests of politicians and organizations. Instead, the likely, even preordained, course of reform is merely different, and perhaps new, ways of dividing the wealth to which the regulatory environment enables access.

However, this does not imply that securities reform legislation necessarily runs counter to the interests of middle-size companies. For instance, the Act's alteration of the applicability of joint and several liability will likely reduce the liability of professional advisors; middle-size companies may benefit through lower costs of equity. The exceptions to the new rule, in the form of minimal plaintiff qualifications and the retained liability of unrelated parties for the insolvency of a largely liable defendant (essentially making all defendants insurers of insolvency risk to plaintiffs) may prove to be so large as to consume the rule.

Similar issues exist as to congressional reform of Rule 9(b) and 11. Real issues do exist as to the applicability of sanctions for frivolous litigation, because some of the most groundbreaking cases in the history of the United States were clear challenges to existing law and frivolous by prevailing standards.[14] It is unlikely, however, that such landmark cases are at issue in the vast majority of securities litigation.

More importantly, these reforms are effected through the vehicle of existing civil procedure-an arguably dilapidated Edsel. In order to utilize the Act's provisions for reform, the defendant must proceed through the judicial system. Under the "old" securities litigation regime, 70 percent of cases were settled out of court, while the company defendants won the vast majority of the remaining 30 percent in court (Stouffer, 1986). This is the classic problem in securities litigation and will not be substantially affected by mere procedural reform; suits are brought by plaintiff attorneys who do not want to win, but to get paid. These suits are brought against companies who do not want to be in court, and usually find it cheaper to simply pay the lawyer to go away.

Given the economies of scale that characterize the legal activities of larger companies, as well as the beneficial effects of their large legal prevention activities, middle-size companies cannot benefit considerably, or even marginally, from the Act's reforms when they still require the middle-size company to spend money on legal defense activities. Benefits to mid-size companies are exceedingly unlikely because mere tinkering with a demonstratedly ineffectual system will not result in dramatic and systemic improvement, except for specific actors who have paid for legislative largesse—usually with other people's money. True reform is in the nature of the eradication of the entire system of mandatory disclosure; that, however, would also mean eradication of pots of potential political contributions—also exceedingly unlikely.

IV. TORT REFORM

Tort reform has become one of the most significant legislative issues at both the state and federal level. The House and Senate have passed tort reform legislation of their own, although no such bill has become law. In the clamor for tort reform, the first and most important issue is the desirability of federal tort reform legislation.

Because legislation is created in a democratic marketplace, federal tort reform cannot be in the ultimate best interests of any interest group, such as mid-size businesses, that do not and likely cannot offer the political system sufficient amounts of political currency. Presently, however, tort reform legislation is a matter for state legislatures. This is in the best interests of disaggregated interest groups, because the transactional costs of obtaining favorable legislation in state and local political arenas to organized interest groups are much higher. When organized interest groups must spend in each of the fifty states, rather than only Washington, it is less likely they will obtain the legislation they seek in every corner of the nation.

The reason to oppose tort reform at the federal level is that mid-size businesses will have a greater voice in state legislatures. Big business dominates policymaking at the federal level.[15] Big business dominates the think tanks that advise government policymakers. Big business and big government are allies;[16] small and mid-size business suffers from this alliance, but small business is organized and can obtain exemptions. While mid-size businesses may not be able to organize to the extent of small businesses—because of dramatically disparate interests—they have a significant voice in local government. States have responded; tort reform has been implemented in several states, and is under consideration in most others.

However, the same issues that plague securities litigation reform also affect tort reform. Most efforts at tort reform operate within the existing and problematic civil procedure regime. The problem is systemic:

Because they are implemented in an adversarial system, changes in procedural rules, even apparently neutral ones, either have surprisingly little impact or only serve to complicate rather than simplify the system.

*   *   *

The reason... reforms derailed is that lawyers, claiming a duty of zealous representation but who are motivated by a desire to run up fees, always can find something to argue about. Change a rule to make it simpler, and adversaries will argue about the interpretation and intent of the new rules, its relation to the old, whether the change is retroactive, whether old precedents apply, whether a judge-made exception should apply, and so on (Toothman, 1995).

An example from Indiana's effort at tort reform is telling. Indiana modified the rules as to the applicability of strict liability in products liability suits. One sentence of Indiana's Product Liability Act provides that a seller will not be strictly liable for defects in a product unless the seller "has actual knowledge of a defect in a product" (Ind. Code § 33-1-1.5-1(A), 1995). This apparently simple exception acquires new meaning in a legal commentary:

Courts will, for example, be required to determine the meaning of "knowledge of a defect".... Is it sufficient to show that the seller knew the product had or lacked a particular feature or must plaintiff prove that the seller knew this condition rendered the product "unreasonably dangerous?" Will sellers be subject to strict liability where they have knowledge that a less expensive model does not have all the options of a more expensive product? (Peterson, 1995.)

States have adopted some changes which affect substantive issues. For example, several states now limit the amount of punitive damages a jury can award. So long as no judicial or lawyerly exceptions are permitted to such changes, genuine reductions in the cost to businesses of the overzealous plaintiff's bar can be effected. At best, however, these are gap-filling measures and really no more than "tinkering" with the system. Genuine reform requires examination of entire judicial systems and the incentives they create; mere modifications to the existing system will benefit discrete, organized interest groups. Disaggregated interest groups might be thrown a scrap from the table in order to reduce opposition—and therefore transactional costs—but certainly cannot expect "optimal" legislation.

An example of the interest-group theory of legislation is the the federal tort "reform" effort directed at the light aircraft industry in the United States. Following World War II, the light aircraft industry in the United States boomed. By 1978-1979, there were twenty-nine manufacturers of light aircraft in the Unites States, including the largest manufacturers, Cessna, Piper, and Beech. These manufacturers produced over 14,000 light aircraft annually, realized annual revenues of over $2 billion, and supported about 560,000 jobs.[17] By 1993, about 500 light aircraft were produced in the United States.[18] (Piper was emerging from Chapter 11 bankruptcy protection and produced 2 percent of their 1978 production; Beech was producing 18 percent of their 1978 production and Cessna had ceased production of light aircraft (McAllister, 1995)). Manufacturers attributed this precipitous decline primarily to their liability for real or imagined design or manufacturing defects in all aircraft, many twenty, thirty, or fourty years old. Spurred by the "big three" light aircraft manufacturers, this "liability tail" became the focus of federal tort reform efforts.[19]

The General Aviation Revitalization Act of 1994[20] (GARA) provided an eighteen-year federal statute of repose on civil actions for death, injury, or damage to property resulting from defective light aircraft or their components over eighteen years old. Essentially, GARA bars claims in tort for airframes or aircraft components that are over eighteen years old. Conspicuously, the American Trial Lawyers Association (ATLA), an organization which represents plaintiffs' attorneys, did not oppose GARA or even appear at any relevant congressional hearings.[21] While ostensibly a boon to the entire light aircraft industry, GARA actually benefits discrete interest groups—the "big three."

GARA will reduce products liability exposure to major manufacturers. However, it is unlikely that these manufacturers will redeploy capital savings to increase R&D or production of light aircraft, because production and sale of turbine and jet aircraft is far more profitable (McAllister, 1995, p. 316). It is

therefore questionable whether GARA will actually revitalize the
light aircraft industry, or allow (formerly) major manufacturers
of light aircraft to expand into more profitability and unrelated
industries. Furthermore, while GARA professedly bars liability of
component manufacturers after eighteen years, components are
replaced on a regular basis (McAllister, 1995, pp. 317-318). Each
component replacement or overhaul resets the eighteen-year
liability exclusion. That is, airframe manufacturers like Cessna,
Piper, and Beech are not liable, generally, once the airframe is
eighteen years old. However, those who manufacture, install, or
maintain airframe components which are replaced or rebuilt at
least several times over eighteen years, such as engines and
avionics, face continual liability. Finally, GARA does not address
the liability of other industry actors, such as maintenance shops
(McAllister, 1995, p. 318). For these reasons, GARA demonstrates
how tort reform at the federal level does not benefit the industry
at large, but rather only discrete, organized, and well-funded
interest groups.

V. GOVERNMENT AND THE FUTURE

There are innumerable anecdotes about the inefficacy and illogic
of government regulatory and tax efforts (see, e.g., Howard, 1994).
Perhaps the most interesting of the lot is the Kansas City bank
that was ordered by regulators to install a Braille keypad at a *drive-
through* ATM at a cost of about $5,000 (Menninger & Margolies,
1995, p. 14). Equally well-known are the firepower of the small-
business lobby and government actions that benefit
megacorporations.

Rather than review these anecdotes, this section will consider
two courses of action that middle-size businesses can take in order
to resist the inevitable results that flow from the interest-group
theory. These courses of action are (1) organization and (2)
operation within the power base.

Organization is relatively straightforward. The ability to
purchase legislation—and the term purchase is not used venally
or perjoratively—is a function of political assets. Political

currency may be campaign contributions, or it may be the ability to mobilize voters. For example, Senator Dole has flown on ADM's private jets 29 times since 1993, for about one-fourth the actual cost (see Weiner, 1996). Archer-Daniels-Midland is an example of a campaign contributor; anti-abortion forces represent mobilized voters, and groups such as the NRA are hybrids among the two.

However, middle-size businesses are handicapped in their organizational efforts because they represent so many disparate interests. Too large to be considered small businesses and too small to be powerful lobbies as individuals, the middle really has only one unifying interest: resistance. Specifically, large and small businesses obtain favors from the government in exchange for political capital. These benefits are paid for by the rest of society which is disaggregated and unable to bargain for nonapplicability. Thus, the only unifying interest among middle-size businesses may be to resist wealth transfer to other interest groups.

But this is a complicated proposition. There is almost no limit to the ingenuity of the politically or monetarily wealthy in extracting wealth from the rest of society. For example, the Tax Reform Act of 1986 was heralded as a defeat for the special interests and as a victory for tax reformers (see Birnbaum & Murray, 1988). In fact, the Tax Reform Act was rife with special interest benefits, although they are not easily revealed by a facile examination. Transition rules such as the "Marriott Amendment" are only one example of hidden wealth transfer mechanisms.[22] It is costly to ferret-out, little yet intercept, wealth transfer legislation of this sort, yet middle-size businesses must do so.

The power base of middle-size business is local. A middle-size business has far more political capital locally and at the state level. This is simply because middle-size businesses contribute considerably to economies at these levels, and because the costs to the interest groups which dominate Washington to monitor and effect all localities and states is prohibitive. For these reasons, middle-size businesses should resist any effort to federalize any issue, such as tort reform, and actively seek to reverse the recent trend toward federal preemption.

Removal of political decision making from Washington to states and localities is akin to the transition in military tactics from the "brute force" approach of World War I to the indirect approach of grand strategy which characterizes modern warfare (see Liddell, 1991). Specifically, middle-size businesses must seek to "fight" on terrain of their own choosing, where the advantages accrue to them. Furthermore, the disparate interests of mid-size business at a national level do not facilitate organization. But at the local level, particularly on such issues as litigation reform, which is—for now—a primarily state concern, middle-sized businesses can mobilize to resist wealth-transferring legislation.

VI. CONCLUSION

Our political-legal system is not corrupt. It is, however, composed of rational individuals and groups acting to maximize their self-interest. Within this system, benefits flow from government to those who are most able to expend political capital to obtain them. Conversely, those who are least able to expend political capital often pay, in the form of wealth transfers, for the benefits that accrue to others. Mid-size business is among the latter group.

It is vital that all political activities, particularly recent litigation reform efforts, be analyzed from this perspective. A characteristic of the reform efforts examined here is that they work no fundamental change on the system; perpetuation of the problematic system cannot fairly be called reform.

Middle-size business can minimize the effect of wealth-transferring legislative actions. To do so, these businesses must find common ground with one another and became actors in the system in those places where their intrinsic nature is most advantageous. The best interests of middle-size businesses are not served by mere acceptance of marginal concessions from organized interest groups. Rather, mid-size businesses ought organize and become informed in order to resist wealth-transferring legislation and to work genuine and fundamental reform.

NOTES

1. Mid-size firms may not issue securities. However, mandatory disclosure and other aspects of the securities regulation regime not only increase the costs of issuing securities, but also increase the cost of capital generally, especially to mid-size firms. This occurs in two ways. First, firms must have a larger sales base in order to cost-effectively amortize issuance costs. Thus, there are more firms that must use forms of capitalization other than the public issue of securities. Second, these costs are, essentially, a tariff on capital. In the presence of a tariff on imported goods, domestic manufacturers of the same goods respond by raising their prices. In the case of a tariff on equity finance, the costs of all competing forms of capitalization, such as commercial lending, will increase. Therefore, while a mid-sized firm may not bear the direct costs of securities regulation, the indirect cost of such regulation—increased costs of all capital—are imposed on all firms regardless of size. Small firms, however, may have lower capital requirements, while larger firms can take advantage of the fixed cost of public equity and realize lower capital costs than mid-size businesses.

2. Of course, in some cases where the plaintiff's claim is apparently meritorious, the defendant may choose to litigate, because the precedent set by an early settlement may be ultimately harmful to the defendant.

3. A defendant could embark on a strategy of intense defensive litigation in hopes of developing a reputation for not settling, in order to deter future plaintiffs. Considering the number of possible plaintiffs, it is unlikely that any mid-size company could afford this strategy for the length of time required to develop the reputation.

4. See Beese (1995), "A large portion of investors never bother to read the material required by law."

5. Sections 11(e), (f) and 15 of the 1933 Act and Section 20(a) of the 1934 Act.

6. 17 C.F.R. § 240.10b-5 (1987). See Kardon v. National Gypsum Co., 69 F. Supp. 512 (E.D. Pa., 1946).

7. See Basic Inc. v. Levinson, 485 U.S. 224, 245 (1988).

8. Senate Panel Hears Views on Reducing Number of Frivolous Rule 10b-5 Actions, Sec. Reg. & L. Rep. (BNA), at par 118 (June 18, 1993).

9. Senate Panel Hears Views on Reducing Number of Frivolous Rule 10b-5 Actions, Sec. Reg. & L. Rep. (BNA), at par 847 (June 18, 1993).

10. Private Securities Litigation Reform Act, Pub. Law 104-67, 109 Stat. 737 (1995). While a recent Supreme Court ruling could arguably be called judicial reform of securities regulations, the holding is so unclear and controversial that it will probably succeed only in generating more litigation in attempts at clarification. In Gustafson v. Alloyd Co., 115 S.Ct. 1061 (1995), the Court considered Section 12(2) of the 1933 Act, which makes liable for damages a seller of securities who misrepresents or omits material facts "by means of a prospectus or oral communication." Although Section 2(10) of the 1933 Act defines a

prospectus very broadly, the Court ignored Section 2(10) and chose to construe "prospectus" in Section 12(2) to mean the same as in Section 10 of the 1933 Act. Section 10 defines "prospectus" as a document "related to a public offering by an issuer or its controlling shareholders." While *Gustafson* will only marginally effect securities litigation, which is primarily brought under Rule 10b-5, the ruling could mark abandonment of the Court's policy that securities laws should be interpreted liberally in order to protect investors. See, for example, Weiss (1995); Bainbridge (1995).

11.   *Congressional Record*, Dec. 5, 1995, p. 17958 (statement of Senator Dodd).

12.   For a description of the public-interest model, see McCormick and Tollison (1981).

13.   See Phillips and Zecher (1981, pp. 21-23), arguing that a well-organized special interest group of securities analysts and institutional investors obtained a regulatory subsidy from the SEC of more than $1 billion when the SEC required securities issuers to supply data in particular formats that the securities analysts and institutional investors otherwise would have had to pay to obtain.

14.   Buffone (1995, p. 678). An example of a landmark case is Brown v. Board of Education, 347 U.S. 483 (1954).

15.   Pearl (1995) discussing telecommunications bills before Congress which include benefits for particular corporations.

16.   See, for example, Georges (1995), noting that President Clinton and his cabinet have refused to support cuts in subsidies to big business.

17.   General Aviation Revitalization Act of 1993, Hearing on H.R. 3087 Before the Subcomm. on Aviation of the House Comm. on Public Works and Transportation, 103d Cong., 1st Sess. 8-12 (1993).

18.   See note 17.

19.   The public rationale for pursuit of federal tort reform, as opposed to reform at the state level, was that "the overarching Federal authority over safety offered the best chance of achieving uniformity of legislation" (McAllister, 1995, p. 309).

20.   General Revitalization Act of 1994, Pub. L. No. 103-298, 1994 U.S.C.C.A.N. 1552.

21.   McAllister (1995, pp. 309-310). ATLA's acquiescence "delivered an ominous message...'GARA satisfies ATLA.'" That GARA satisfied ATLA certainly questions the efficacy of GARA as a tort "reform" effort, because ATLA, in general, maintains that our society has in the past sacrificed safety to economic growth and industrial prosperity, and that stricter standards of care as to products liability offers needed legal redress. Of course, stricter products liability standards certainly would also benefit plaintiffs' lawyers.

22.   The Marriott Amendment is an exception to a provision that limits business meal and entertainment deductions to 80 percnet of the actual expense. To qualify for the exception, a convention must include a speaker whenever food and beverages are included in the program. See I.R.C. § 274(n)(3)(D). The

sponsor was Senator Dole, who was a frequent and well-compensated speaker at such events. See Doernberg and McChesney (1987).

REFERENCES

15 U.S.C. § 77 (1988).

15 U.S.C. §§ 78a-7811 (1988 & Supp. 1993).

17 C.F.R. § 230.251-.262 (1995).

17 C.F.R. § 230.501-.508 (1995).

17 C.F.R. § 240.10b-5 (1987).

Arthur Andersen & Co. et al. (1992). *The liability crisis in the United States: Impact on the accounting profession.*

Bainbridge, S,M. (1995). Securities act section 12(2) after the gustafson debacle. *Business Law, 50,* 1231.

Basic Inc. v. Levinson. (1988). 485 U.S. 224.

Beese, Jr., J.C. (1995, September 9). Confessions of a securities regulator. *Wall Street Journal,* p. A23.

Birnbaum, J.H., & Murray, A.S. (1988). *Showdown at Gucci gulch.*

Boenninghausen, M.V. (1993, November 15). Bill would limit securities suits. *N.J.L.J.,* p. 30.

Brown v. Board of Education, 347 U.S. 483 (1954).

Buffone, D.C. (1995). Predatory attorneys and professional plaintiffs: Reforms are needed to limit vexatious securities litigation, *Hofstra Law Review, 23,* p. 655.

Burton, L. (1992, March 3). Legal liability awards are frightening smaller CPA firms away from audits. *Wall Street Journal,* p. B1.

Congressional Record. (1995, December 5). Statement of Senator Dodd, p. 17958.

Doernberg, R.L., & McChesney, F.S. (1987). Doing good or doing well? Congress and the tax reform act of 1986. *New York University Law Review, 62,* p. 891.

Fama, E.F. (1970). Efficient capital markets: A review of theory and empirical work, *Journal Finance, 25,* p. 383.

General Revitalization Act of 1994. (1994). Pub. L. No. 103-298, 1994 *U.S.C.C.A.N.,* p. 1552.

General Aviation Revitalization Act of 1993. (1993). Hearing on H.R. 3087 Before the Subcommittee on Aviation of the House Committee on Public Works and Transportation, 103rd Congress, 1st Session, pp. 8-12.

Georges, C. (1995, March 7). Subsidies and tax breaks for business are targeted for cuts by broad alliance. *Wall Street Journal,* p. A21.

Gustafson v. Alloyd Co. (1995). 115 S.Ct. 1061.

Hamilton, J. (1996, January 10). Private securities litigation reform act of 1995. *Federal Sec. Law Rep., 1696,* 28.

Liddell Hart, B.H. (1991). *Strategy.*

Howard, P.K. (1994). *The death of common sense.*

Indiana Code. (1995). § 33-1-1.5-1(A).

I.R.C. § 274(n)(3)(D).

Junewicz, J.J., & Hildebrand, D.G. (1995). Recent developments in securities class action and shareholder derivative suits: A review of legal reform legislation and significant cases *4. *Practising Law Institute No. B4-7086.*

Kardon v. National Gypsum Co. (1946). *Federal Supplement, 69,* 512 (E.D. Pa. 1946).

Lerarch, W.S. (1995, April 19). Prevalence and economic impact of securities class actions: Is reform necessary? *Practising Law Institute Handbook.*

Macey, J.R. (1994). Administrative agency obsolescence and interest group Formation: A case study of the SEC at sixty. *Cardozo Law Review, 15,* 909.

Markowitz, H. (1952). Portfolio selection. *Journal of Finance, 7,* 77.

McAllister, T.S. (1952). A "tail" of liability reform: General aviation revitalization act of 1994 & the general aviation industry in the United states, *Transportation Law Journal, 23,* 301.

McCormick, R.E., & Tollison, R.D. (1981). *Politicians, legislation, and the economy: An inquiry into the interest group theory of government.*

Mehta, S.N., & Selz, M. (1995, June 15). Steps are taken to ease the burdens of complying with federal regulations. *Wall Street Journal,* p. B2.

Menninger, B., & Margolies, D. (1995, January 13). Regulatory overkill is smothering businesses. *Wichita Business Journal,* p. 14.

Note. (1993). The SEC's small business initiatives and regulation A: New life for an old exemption. *Journal of Law & Commerce, 13,* 157.

Pashigian, B.P. (1982). A theory of prevention and legal defense with an application to the legal costs of companies. *Journal of Law & Economics, 25,* 247.

Pearl, D. (1995, December 12). Telecommunications bill looks fashioned to fit. *Wall Street Journal,* p. A22.

Peterson, J.L. (1995, September). Tort reform. *Res Gestae,* p. 25.

Phillips, S.M., & Zecher, J.R. (1981). *The SEC and the public interest.*

Policzer, M. (1992, April 27). They've cornered the market: A few firms dominate the derivative-suit arena. *National Law Journal,* 1.

Private Securities Litigation Reform Act. (1995). Public Law 104-67, 109 Statute 737.

Selz, M. (1994, February 2). Regulatory pressure on banks benefit small businesses. *Wall Street Journal,* p. B2.

Senate panel hears views on reducing number of frivolous rule 10b-5 actions. (1993, June 18.). *Sec. Reg. & L. Rep,* (BNA), par 118.

Sharpe, W.F. (1964). Capital asset prices: A theory of market equilibrium under conditions of risk. *Journal of Finance, 19,* 425.

Siconolfi, M., & Raghaven, A. (1995, August 22). Securities firms make large gifts to congressmen. *Wall Street Journal*, p. C1.

Stouffer, R. (1986, August 25). Litigation explosion 'Booming.' *Pittsburgh Business Times & Journal*, p. 5.

Toothman, J.W. (1995, September). Real reform. *A.B.A.J.*, 80.

Weidenbaum, M. (1996, March 1). *The overlooked middle: Government regulation and medium-size business.* Paper presented at FINOVA Policy Conference on Mid-Sized Business.

Weiner, T. (1996, January 16). Dwayne's world. *New York Times*, p. D1.

Weiss, E.J. (1995). *Securities act section 12(2) after Gustafson v. Alloyd Company: What questions remain? Business Law, 50,* 1210.

Witnesses dispute whether reform needed to stem spurious litigation. (1993, July 26). *Banking Republic (BNA)*, p. 121.

FISCAL POLICIES AND
MID-SIZE BUSINESS

James Alm

I. INTRODUCTION

These are turbulent times for national economic policies, with a
dizzying array of policy changes under consideration by those in
Washington. Especially volatile are fiscal policies. In the past year
Congress has made attempts to balance the budget, it has acted
upon a number of laws that change specific tax features in the
tax code, and legislators have introduced an unprecedented
number of bills that propose basic and fundamental reforms in
our nation's tax laws.

These fiscal policies, if ultimately passed into law, promise to
have profound effects on the nation's economy, and their possible
impacts have been the subject of extensive analyses. However,

Advances in the Study of Entrepreneurship, Innovation, and Economic Growth,
Volume 8, pages 57-97.
Copyright © 1996 by JAI Press Inc.
All rights of reproduction in any form reserved.
ISBN: 0-7623-0185-6

this debate has largely focused on the effects of these policies on individual behavior: will individuals work more with fiscal reforms, will they save and invest more, will they report more income, how will their costs of complying with the tax laws be affected, how will the distribution of income be affected, will individual behavioral changes affect such things as interest rates and the growth rate of the economy, and the like. Also present, although to a lesser extent, are similar questions about the responses of the "business" sector. However, the business sector is often portrayed as a single, homogeneous group. Alternatively, only its extremes—the very large or the very small businesses— are sometimes examined. As noted by Weidenbaum (1996), largely absent in these analyses is discussion about the effects on the "overlooked middle" sector of American business. These firms have revenues that range from $10 million to $300 million, and they exist in all sectors of the economy: agriculture, construction, manufacturing, transportation, wholesale and retail trade, finance, and services. They also have a variety of organizational structures, from proprietorships to partnerships to corporations. In total, they constitute a significant proportion of the American economy, in their shares of total jobs, sales, assets, and, importantly, taxes.

In this chapter I discuss the specific form that recent federal government fiscal policies has taken in the United States, and examine their likely effects on "Mid-Size Business" (MSB). In particular, I examine three sets of fiscal policies: deficit reduction, some specific or piecemeal tax changes (e.g., relief for the alternative minimum tax, extension of expiring tax provisions, cuts in capital gains tax rates), and, especially, fundamental tax reform. The analysis focuses upon how MSB will be affected by these policy changes, who gains and loses from them, and whether these effects are desirable. I also discuss the general form that federal government tax policy should take toward MSB.

It should be obvious that there are a number of dimensions of fiscal policies that I cannot discuss. One focus here is on federal government policies, even though those of state and local governments also have important impacts on businesses. Another focus is on the effects of fiscal policies on MSB; the effects on individuals and other businesses are largely ignored, except to the extent that these responses are relevant to MSB, and the effects of other policies such as regulation and litigation reforms are also ignored.[1]

The next section presents some summary information on federal government tax treatment of MSB. The following sections discuss recent efforts to reduce the federal government deficit, some specific tax proposals that affect MSB, and then more basic tax reform suggestions. Some tentative suggestions for fiscal reforms are made in the final section.

II. FEDERAL TAX TREATMENT OF MID-SIZE BUSINESS

It is useful at the start to examine a number of federal government tax provisions that currently affect business, including MSB. Table 1 lists the amount of corporate income taxes paid by all corporations in 1992, the most recent year for which detailed information is available. Also listed in Table 1 are my estimates of the amount of the tax paid by MSB. These latter estimates assume that MSB are primarily those corporations whose asset sizes in 1992 range from $5 million to $250 million; within these ranges the annual revenues of the firms average from $13 million to $96 million. Note that the estimates of MSB taxes in Table 1 do not include taxes paid by proprietorships, partnerships, or *S* corporations. The average sizes of such businesses are typically smaller than the sizes of MSB, although there are obviously many exceptions.

Table 1 indicates that MSB generate 24 percent of total corporate sector revenues, earn 15 percent of the net income, and pay 16 percent of total corporate taxes (or 18 percent of total taxes after credits). Table 1 also presents evidence that the average effective tax rate on MSB (or total income tax after credits divided by net income) ranges from 25 to 37 percent, with some tendency to rise and then fall with greater asset size. The average tax rate for all corporations is 25 percent, and there is some tendency for both smaller and larger corportions to face a lower average tax rate than MSB. Note that corporate income tax revenues were

Table 1. Corporate Income Tax Collections

Item	Total	Size of Total Assets[a]				
		1 to 100,000	100,000 to 250,000	250,000 to 500,000	500,000 to 1,000,000	1,000,000 to 5,000,000
Number of Returns	3,869,023	1,986,072	628,341	384,301	260,281	270,840
Total Assets[b]	20,002,094	61,308	101,334	136,393	183,336	566,301
Total Receipts[b]	11,742,135	363,567	311,446	332,738	394,206	1,209,910
Total Net Income[b]	401,997	2,009	2,754	3,389	3,821	14,453
Total Income Tax[b]	131,285	366	545	675	1,053	3,702
Total Income Tax after Credits[b]	101,532	357	534	650	1,024	3,531
Average Assets[c]	5,170	31	161	355	704	2,091
Average Receipts[c]	3,035	183	496	866	1,515	4,467
Average Net Income[c]	103	1.01	4.38	8.82	15	53
Average Income Tax[c]	34	0.18	0.87	1.76	4.05	14
Average Income Tax after Credits[c]	26	0.18	0.85	1.69	3.93	13
Average Effective Tax Rate[d]	25.3%	17.8%	19.4%	19.2%	26.8%	24.4%

(continued)

Table 1. (Continued)

Item	Size of Total Assets[a]					
	5,000,000 to 10,000,000	10,000,000 to 25,000,000	25,000,000 to 50,000,000	50,000,000 to 100,000,000	100,000,000 to 250,000,000	Above 250,000,000
Number of Returns	38,176	24,544	11,153	7,720	6,227	6,269
Total Assets[b]	264,806	382,563	396,552	546,184	983,425	16,379,893
Total Receipts[b]	515,844	590,604	409,095	389,452	595,788	6,484,488
Total Net Income[b]	7,757	11,810	8,170	11,092	21,436	315,569
Total Income Tax[b]	2,099	3,296	3,322	4,357	7,436	103,006
Total Income Tax after Credits[b]	2,000	3,047	3,014	3,769	6,315	75,910
Average Assets[c]	6,936	15,587	35,556	70,749	157,929	2,612,840
Average Receipts[c]	1,351	24,063	36,680	50,447	95,678	1,034,374
Average Net Income[c]	203	481	733	1,437	3,442	50,338
Average Income Tax[c]	55	134	298	564	1,194	16,431
Average Income Tax after Credits[c]	52	124	270	488	1,014	12,109
Average Effective Tax Rate[d]	25.8%	25.8%	36.9%	34.0%	29.5%	24.1%

Notes: [a] Asset sizes are in dollar amounts.
[b] Dollar amounts are in millions of dollars.
[c] Dollar amounts are in thousands of dollars.
[d] The Average Effective Tax Rate (expressed as a percentage) is calculated by dividing Income Tax after Credits by Net Income.

Source: Internal Revenue Service (1995).

9 percent of total federal government tax collections in 1992; this percentage has risen to nearly 12 percent in 1995.

Taxes *paid* by MSB are clearly an important part of federal tax policy toward MSB. Also important are taxes *not paid*. Table 2 lists Congressional Budget Office (CBO) (1995a) estimates of the magnitude of several of the more important "tax expenditures" affecting business.[2] Tax expenditures measure the amount by which tax revenues are reduced by the special provisions of the tax code. In total, the major tax expenditure items generated tax savings in excess of $50 billion in 1995. The largest of these items is accelerated depreciation of equipment and buildings. Other important tax expenditure items include the tax savings from the graduated corporate income tax rate structure, the tax credit for corporations with income from United States possessions, and the exception to the source rule for the sale of inventory property. A more disaggregate analysis of business tax expenditures indicates that the different business sectors— agriculture, manufacturing, mining, utilities, transportation, finance, trades/services, communications, and construction— receive very different amounts of support.

It is, however, essential to remember that the identification either of tax burdens or tax expenditures does not necessarily mean that it is the business that is the ultimate recipient of the cost or the benefit of the program. Economists have tried over the years to identify who bears the burden of taxation, but the incidence of the corporate income tax and its many provisions remains particularly elusive. There are four possible candidates who might pay the corporate tax burden: the owners of the corporations, the recipients of capital income from any and all sources, the individuals who supply their resources to the corporation, the consumers of corporate products. Many economists believe that the most likely candidate for the corporate tax burden, at least in the long run, is all those individuals who own capital (Kotlikoff & Summers, 1987). However, this conclusion is not universally held even among economists, let alone among those who run the corporations.

Table 2.   Federal Government Tax Expenditures, 1995
(Amounts in billions of dollars)

Tax Provision	Amount
Depreciation of equipment in excess of alternative depreciation system	25.6
Depreciation of buildings other than rental housing in excess of alternative depreciation system	4.9
Reduced rates on first $10 million of corporate taxable income	3.9
Tax credit for corporations with income from U.S. possessions (Section 936 income)	3.7
Exception to the source rule for the sale of inventory property	3.5
Tax credit for low-income housing	2.2
Special treatment of life insurance companies' reserves	2.1
Expensing of research and development costs	2.0
Deduction of unpaid property loss reserves for property and casualty insurance companies	1.6
Expensing of up to $17,500 of depreciable business property	1.5
Exclusion of income of foreign sales corporations	1.4
Deferral of income of controlled foreign corporations	1.1
Credit for increasing research activities	1.1
Credit for producing nonconventional fuels	1.1

Source: Congressional Budget Office (1995a).

It is also important to remember that there are many tax expenditures that are directed to individuals through the individual income tax that nonetheless have profound impacts on business. The most obvious of these is the deductibility of mortgage interest payments on owner-occupied housing, as well as the excludability of net imputed rental income on such housing. These provisions generated total tax expenditures (for individuals) of nearly $75 billion in 1995; both provisions clearly stimulate the demand for housing.

III.   DEFICIT REDUCTION

A central thrust of national fiscal policy this last year has been to move the federal government over a period of time to a balanced budget. For every fiscal year since 1969, the federal government has spent more than it has collected in taxes. At this time it appears that the efforts to pass a comprehensive and multiyear balanced budget plan have failed, although it seems likely that some limited agreement between Congress and the White House will eventually be reached that involves the passage of a single year's budget, if not the passage of a balanced budget.[3]

A.   The Current and Projected Magnitude of Federal Deficits

Table 3 presents some recent information on the federal deficits, both now and in the near future. The deficit in 1995 totaled $164 billion, and is projected by the Congressional Budget Office (1995b) to increase to well over $300 billion by the year 2002 in the absence of any discretionary fiscal policy changes. Congress has passed a budget (the Balanced Budget Reconciliation Act of 1995) that would have led to a balanced budget by the year 2002, according to projections, but this bill was vetoed by the President late in 1995. Intensive negotiations between Congress and the White House have led to some agreements on specific budgetary items, but to date no comprehensive agreement has been reached. In early February 1996 the President submitted a budget that would lead to a balanced budget in the year 2001, but the outcome of this budget is highly uncertain at this time.

Table 3.   Current and Projected Federal Government Deficits (Dollar amounts in billions of dollars)

	1994	1995	1996	1997	1998	1999	2000	2001	2002
Expenditures									
Administration	1461	1519	1572	1635	1676	1717	1761	1812	1868
Congress	—	—	1568	1609	1644	1685	1738	1779	1836
CBO Baseline	—	—	1602	1686	1766	1873	1982	2087	2211
Revenues									
Administration	1258	1355	1427	1495	1578	1653	1734	1820	1912
Congress	—	—	1417	1450	1518	1588	1666	1745	1839
CBO Baseline	—	—	1413	1468	1537	1612	1694	1779	1870
Deficit									
Administration	203	164	146	140	98	64	28	(8)	(44)
Congress	—	—	151	159	127	97	73	34	(3)
CBO Baseline	—	—	189	218	229	261	288	308	340

Sources: *Budget of the United States Government, Fiscal Year 1997;* Balanced Budget Reconciliation Act of 1995; and Congressional Budget Office (1995b).

An important issue to consider is the benefits and costs of a balanced budget. More precisely, why is it necessary or desirable to achieve a budget in which government expenditures equal tax revenues? It turns out that there is a surprising amount of disagreement among economists about the economic impact of large budget deficits. Let me consider the different views, ignoring until later the specific means (e.g., expenditure cuts versus tax increases) by which a balanced budget would be achieved.

B.   Views on Deficits[4]

The Keynesian View

Most economists agree that there are at least some circumstances under which deficits are actually desirable. This perspective on deficits (sometimes called the "Keynesian View") is based on the fact that the size of the deficit depends upon two basic elements: discretionary tax and expenditure decisions, and the performance of the economy. When the economy moves into a recession, government expenditures automatically increase and revenues automatically decrease, due to the presence of automatic stabilizers in the federal budget. Consequently, the deficit increases in such periods, even if the government takes no direct action on spending or taxes. Similarly, the deficit declines as the economy expands, again with no discretionary decisions by government. These automatic changes in the "cyclical deficit" are viewed favorably by most economists because the economy is stimulated when there is need for stimulus and restrained when there is need for restraint. However, if the deficit remains even when the economy is at full employment—a situation that currently exists—then such a deficit is called a "structural deficit." Here the evaluation of deficits is considerably more controversial.

The Neoclassical View

In the "Neoclassical View" of deficits, structural deficits are seen as the source of a variety of economic ills. The most frequently mentioned negative effect of deficits emphasizes its impact on interest rates and, through that channel, on private investment. Remember that a deficit occurs when the government borrows from the public to finance its expenditures. This borrowing is done by the Treasury Department, which issues government debt and so competes with other borrowers for the available loanable funds. Increased government demand for credit therefore puts upward pressure on interest rates and so crowds out private investors competing for the same funds. In the long run these deficits therefore reduce the private capital stock, which lowers economic growth and future standards of living. This channel is the source of the often-heard complaint that "the deficit is mortgaging our children's future." Put differently, the presence of government deficits means that public saving is negative, so that total national saving (or public plus private saving) is reduced.

Of course, the crucial—and often neglected—question here is how the government uses the funds that it has attracted at the expense of private borrowing. If the government invests the funds in productive capital, then the deficit leads to a substitution of public sector capital for private sector capital, and the burden on future generations is accordingly reduced; in fact, if public sector capital is more productive than the displaced private sector capital, then the deficit actually makes future generations better off. There is some limited evidence on the productivity of public infrastructure investments (Hulten & Schwab, 1991). However, most recent federal deficits do not appear to have contributed in any significant way to such investments.

Another adverse effect of deficits stems from their impact on export sectors. To the extent that Treasury borrowing increases domestic interest rates, American investments appear more attractive to foreign investors, and capital flows from abroad to the United States. These capital inflows in turn increase the demand for dollars, and the dollar appreciates relative to other major currencies. A more valuable dollar enables American consumers to buy foreign goods more cheaply; however, it also makes it more difficult for American businesses to sell their products overseas. Deficits therefore crowd out American exporters, which leads to a loss of employment and income in export sectors of the American economy. Unlike the case of investment, there is substantial empirical evidence to support this argument.

When the debt issued to finance the deficit is held overseas, an additional burden emerges. The servicing of debt requires that interest on the debt be paid and that the principal ultimately be retired. When these payments are made abroad, they constitute a transfer from American citizens to individuals living overseas, thereby reducing the living standards of those Americans that must make the payments. Current and future generations are now burdened because current consumption increases at the expense of future consumption.

One last adverse consequence of deficits stems not so much from the deficit per se but from pressure that the existence of the deficit is thought to bring to bear on the government. One pressure is imposed on the monetary authority. There is some fear that large, persistent budget deficits may eventually force the Federal Reserve system to monetize the debt; that is, the Treasury may borrow from the Federal Reserve system rather than from the public, and the monetary authority may pay for the debt that it purchases by printing money. The result of this monetization is a growth in the money supply, and so an increase in inflation. Although this monetization has not occurred in the United States, it has been a fairly common experience in other countries, especially those that have tried to repudiate large debts by inflation.

Another pressure is on the Treasury itself. The presence of a large deficit may lead to government default on the debt, if limitations on the ability of the government to issue new debt imply that the deficit cannot be serviced. Indeed, public discussion of the risk of default has been quite extensive in recent months, although this risk seems to have been substantially overstated by government spokespeople.

In sum, many economists believe that deficits are harmful primarily because some individuals and sectors are burdened now by increased government borrowing, and because future generations are burdened both by the involuntary taxes that they must pay to service the principal and the interest on the debt and also by the smaller capital stock that they receive from the current generation.

The Ricardian View

However, there are other economists who believe that these adverse consequences are both unsubstantiated and unjustified, or who believe that deficits are primarily a symptom rather than a cause of the economic ills that are mistakenly attributed to deficits. These economists make several arguments.

The first argument is that tax and deficit finance are equivalent, in that the burden of each is on current, not future, generations. This argument was first made by David Ricardo over 150 years (hence the name, the "Ricardian View" of deficits), and more recently has been argued by Barro (1989). It rests on the notion that individuals should recognize, when the deficit increases by $1, that their future taxes must also eventually increase by $1 in present value terms, since the $1 of additional debt requires debt service of $1 over its lifetime. If individuals recognize that deficits now require taxes later, then tax and debt finance are equivalent ways of financing government expenditures and so have the same effects. In both cases, the burden is felt by generations at the time the expenditure is made.

However, the assumptions upon which the Ricardian View is based are quite restrictive. These assumptions include: individuals are infinitely lived (or are linked to all future generations by altruistically motivated transfers), there are perfect capital markets, there is no uncertainty, individuals are rational and farsighted, and all taxes are nondistortionary, or lumpsum, taxes. There is little doubt that these assumptions do not hold in the "real" world.

A second argument is that the empirical evidence on the harmful effects of deficits is largely inconclusive; in particular, empirical evidence only weakly supports the link between greater deficits and higher interest rates (Seater, 1993). It appears that many other factors (e.g., the overall state of the economy, the rate of inflation, monetary policy, international trade and financial developments, and so on) interact to determine the level of interest rates. Neither the amount of the deficit nor the amount of the outstanding accumulated debt appears to be a major factor in the determination of interest rates.

A third argument sees deficits as a symptom rather than a cause of economic problems. The notion here is that the government can finance any given level of its expenditures by taxing, by borrowing money from the public, or by expanding the money supply. Although the composition of finance is of some importance, the more crucial issue is the level of spending that must be financed. According to this argument, all the adverse consequences that are attributed to deficits are in fact due to excessive levels of government expenditures, not to the deficit itself.

Summary

This debate is not resolved. The United States has until recently had only a limited experience with large peacetime deficits, and research has only begun to address some of the issues raised in the above discussion. However, my own view, and, I believe, that of the clear majority of economists is that deficits create major problems for the economy, problems that may not appear in their most severe form until several years have passed.

The performance of the United States economy during the Reagan Administration of the 1980s plays a large role in this conclusion. During this eight-year period the federal government spent nearly $1.5 billion more than it collected in tax revenues, leading to a tripling in its outstanding debt. In brief, this experience suggests several general conclusions (Friedman, 1993). First, greater government deficits did not lead to greater private saving; indeed, consumption as a percent of Gross Domestic Product (GDP) increased significantly and total national saving as a percent of GDP decreased significantly over this period. Second, deficits were at the least associated with higher real interest rates. Third, they also resulted in lower private investment. Fourth, greater federal government deficits led to a deterioration in the American trade balance. Finally, deficits resulted in lower net investment, as the American economy was transformed from a capital-exporting to a capital-importing country. In short, the experience of the economy over this period is largely consistent with the predictions of the Neoclassical View, and points to the rejection of the Ricardian View of deficits.

The cumulative impacts on the economy of such deficits are likely to have been substantial. Some of the larger estimates have been made by Ball and Mankiw (1995), who calculate that total output of the American economy is 3 to 6 percent lower than it would have been in the absence of these large fiscal deficits. Other economists estimate considerably smaller impacts.

C.   The Impact of Deficit Reduction on Mid-Size Business

Given that one grants the validity of the Neoclassical View of deficits, what are the effects on MSB of continued, large federal budget deficits? Conversely, how would MSB be affected if a balanced budget was eventually to be passed? Let me focus on the latter question. The answer to this question depends largely on two issues. First, what are the specific means by which a balanced budget will be achieved (e.g., which taxes will be increased and which expenditures will be cut)? Second, how will a balanced budget affect the economy (e.g., saving, investment, interest rates) and, through these impacts, affect in turn MSB?

At this point it is impossible to determine the specific measures that would be contained in the passage of a balanced budget. There are significant, if narrowing, differences between the White House and Congress on the path to budget balance. The original budget passed by Congress and vetoed by the President called for: $271 billion in reductions in the projected growth in Medicare, $163 billion from Medicaid, $13 billion from agricultural programs, $82 billion from welfare programs, $33 billion from the Earned Income Tax Credit, $5 billion from student loans, $5 billion from banking and housing programs, $20 billion in tax increases on businesses, and $245 billion in tax cuts (including a $500 tax credit for each child, an offset for the "marriage penalty," various tax deductions, a retroactive reduction in the capital gains tax rate for individuals and corporations, relief from estate taxes and the corporate alternative minimum tax, and an increase in small business write-off for equipment purchases). The most recent Clinton budget calls for: $297 billion in reductions in the projected growth in various discretionary spending programs, $124 billion from Medicare, $59 billion from Medicaid, $40 billion from welfare programs, $49 billion from several mandatory programs, and $100 billion in tax cuts. However, part of the Clinton deficit reduction occurs by eliminating some corporate tax preferences; these provisions would generate $44 billion in additional revenues, including $5 billion from reformulating the foreign tax credit, $4 billion from disallowing interest deductions on corporate-owned life insurance policies, $4 billion from requiring average-cost basis for stocks and securities, and $3 billion from modifying loss carryback and carryforward provisions. It should be noted that these budget estimates seem to change almost daily.

At present there is some overlap between the White House and the Congressional plans, and some agreement on these common items seems likely. In fact, in many respects the differences between the respective Congressional and White House budgets have narrowed substantially during the budget negotiations. Both parties now agree on significant savings in Medicare, Medicaid, welfare, tax cuts for individuals, and tax increases for corporations; both parties also agree on the use of CBO calculations; and they agree on the need for reaching budget balance by the year 2002. Still, the prospects for a comprehensive multiyear budget agreement remain uncertain.

Even the impact of a balanced budget on MSB is highly uncertain. The most obvious channel by which MSB would be affected is through any changes in interest rates that would occur with the passage of balanced budget. It is widely expected that a balanced budget would lead to lower interest rates, which would reduce business borrowing costs, raise profits, and raise business taxes. Especially affected would be those businesses with large amounts of debt, and those with aggressive plans for capital expansion. However, the interest rate effect cannot be known with certainty. Current CBO analysis projects that short-term interest rates would drop by over 1 percentage point to 3.9 percent, while the yield on 10-year Treasury notes would drop slightly to 5.5 percent. Some private economists project larger or smaller reductions. The impact on MSB of specific provisions in any budget plan cannot be known until more budget details become available.

IV. PIECEMEAL FISCAL CHANGES

A number of specific tax policy changes have been suggested over the last year, although their legislative status remains murky because of the ongoing budget disagreement between Congress and the President. In this section I discuss some of the more important piecemeal fiscal policies that have emerged as possible candidates for passage. My discussion is necessarily selective and brief.

Among the more important provisions that have been suggested in the last year by Congress and the White House as candidates for tax reform are:

- Provision of relief for the alternative minimum tax (AMT). Congress has passed legislation that provides relief for the AMT. As discussed later, the AMT is a major contributor to the compliance costs of the corporate income tax.
- Pensions reversions. Congress has passed legislation that permits firms to transfer excess assets from defined-benefit plans to the employer.
- Elimination of deductibility for corporate-owned life insurance (COLI) Loans. Congress has passed legislation that eliminates the deductibility of interest on COLI loans.
- Repeal of the possessions credit. Congress has passed legislation that repeals the tax credit that allows corporations to offset some of their domestic tax liability on income from business operations in American possessions.
- Extension of expiring provisions. Congress has passed legislation that would extend through 1997 the work opportunity credit, the exclusion for employer-provided educational assistance, the modified research credit, contributions of appreciated stock to private foundations, and the orphan drug credit, among other provisions.
- Reform of depreciation provisions for property. Congress has passed this legislation.
- Phase-out of tax deferral for farm corporations with an accrual method of accounting. Congress has passed this legislation.

- Reform of gain recognition on some extraordinary dividends. Congress has passed this legislation.
- Modification of the basis adjustment rules of Section 1033. Congress has passed this legislation.
- Requirement for some corporate tax shelter registration. Congress has passed this legislation.
- Limitation of loss carrybacks and extension of loss carryforwards. The White House has proposed this legislation.
- Denial of the interest-deduction for corporate debt instruments that carry a term of more than 40 years or that are convertible to stock. The White House has proposed this legislation.
- Reduction of the dividends-received deduction for corporations that own less than 20 percent of the stock of an American corporation. The White House has proposed this legislation.
- Elimination of the lower of cost or market method and the cost of components method in inventory valuation. The White House has proposed this legislation.

At this time, none of these provisions has been enacted into law. Numerous other proposals have also been suggested.

One provision that does not fit neatly into this discussion is the tax treatment of capital gains. One part of the Republican Contract with America calls for the reduction in the maximum tax rate on realized capital gains to 19.8 percent for individuals, with a similar though smaller reduction for businesses. At present these reductions have not been enacted into law. Nevertheless, changes in capital gains taxation are an important part of the recent tax debate, and the case for and against changes merits discussion.

The taxation of capital gains has changed frequently over the last twenty years, and the effects of these changes have been the subject of an intense and unresolved debate. There is strong evidence that changes in the tax treatment of capital gains have a major impact on the timing of short-term realizations. One piece of historical evidence comes from the Tax Reform Act of 1986

(TRA86). As part of TRA86, the preferential treatment of long-term realized capital gains was eliminated as of the 1st of January in 1986. In response, there was an enormous surge in realizations from $166 billion in 1985 to $325 billion in 1986, after which the realizations returned to their pre-1986 levels.

However, the impact of a permanent reduction in capital gains taxation on the sustained level of realizations is far less certain. Recent estimates by Burman and Randolph (1994) suggest that the response to a permanent cut is far less than the response to a temporary cut. In contrast, other economists (Feldstein et al., 1980) conclude that even the sustained level of realizations is quite sensitive to the tax rate.

These estimates are of immense importance in the debate on capital gains tax rate reductions. Advocates of reductions argue that the response of capital gains realizations to tax rate cuts is large and persistent. As a result, they argue further that the cuts will generate such a surge in realizations that tax revenues will actually increase, thereby paying for themselves. Other beneficial results include an increase in personal savings because of the greater return on investments, an increase in investment and risk-taking, the creation of more and more productive jobs, and a higher rate of economic growth. However, if the response of realizations is in fact small and temporary, then the case for tax rate reductions is considerably weakened.

Unfortunately, the evidence is, I believe, inconclusive. The difficulty in resolving the capital gains conundrum also has implications for fundamental tax reform, as discussed next.

V.   FUNDAMENTAL TAX REFORM

Instead of piecemeal changes in specific taxes, another approach to fiscal policy is fundamental tax reform, or changes in the basic structure of taxation imposed by the federal government. There is increasing interest in such an approach, due largely to changing attitudes toward federal income taxation both of corporations and of individuals. The existence of legal and illegal means to reduce tax liabilities has led to the widespread belief that many individuals and businesses do not pay their "fair" share of taxes. High and increasing marginal tax rates and countless special provisions in the tax code have generated numerous distortions in individual and corporate behavior, and there is much concern that the current tax system unduly favors consumption over saving, thereby lowering the growth potential of the economy. The complexity of the tax code has imposed substantial compliance costs on individuals and businesses in the calculation of their taxes, and has also created significant costs for the government in the administration of the taxes. In short, the current form of income taxation is now seen as an inequitable, inefficient, and costly means of raising revenues, and calls for either its reform or replacement are common.

Many proposals for fundamental tax reform have been presented in Congress. Most are intended to replace the existing individual and corporate income taxes, although each could also be viewed as a supplement to these existing taxes. The reform proposals include:

- the Nunn-Domenici Unlimited Savings Allowance (USA) tax system, which combines a flat-rate value-added tax on businesses with a graduated tax on individual consumption expenditures with some allowable personal deductions
- the Boren-Danforth business activities tax, essentially a national value-added tax
- the Lugar and Schaefer versions of a national retail sales tax
- the Hall-Rabushka, Forbes, and Armey-Shelby variants of a "flat tax," which combines a flat-rate tax on business income net of investment, materials, and labor expenses with a flat-rate tax on individual wage income with personal allowances but without deductions.

There are also a number of other reform proposals that modify some features of the existing tax (e.g., the Gephardt "10 Percent Tax").

Now there are essentially two main issues that are commingled in these reforms. *First*, what structure of tax rates should be chosen? Nearly all suggestions for tax reform call for an overall

reduction in marginal tax rates. However, there is much
controversy about whether the rate structure should retain some
of the progressivity that has always characterized income taxation
in the United States, or whether a single, flat rate (imposed on
all income above some level) should be chosen. There is also much
controversy about whether the rate reductions would generate
more or less revenues. *Second*, what tax base should be chosen?
Taxes can be imposed on essentially any of three tax bases:
income (and its component parts, such as wages), consumption
(and its components parts), or wealth. The United States has since
1913 imposed a major tax at the federal government level on
income, somewhat comprehensively defined. However, as noted
above, there is a widespread and growing belief that income
taxation in the United States is responsible for a number of
serious problems, and this belief has generated support for
alternative bases of taxation.

It is important to distinguish between these two issues, or
between the selection of a tax *rate* schedule and the choice of a
base for taxation. Let me discuss each issue separately, but let me
begin with a discussion of some of the problems with the existing
income tax, focusing on the effects on MSB.

A.   Some Problems with the Income Tax

Compliance Costs

A first problem with the income tax is its complexity. The
difficulties that individuals face in determining their taxes have
received widespread publicity. The obstacles that businesses face
are at least as severe. There is abundant anecdotal evidence that
illustrates the magnitude of the problem. For example, executives
recently released the Mobil Corporation's 1993 federal corporate
income tax "return," which consisted of nine volumes containing
6,300 pages, weighing 76 pounds, and costing $10 million to
prepare. Work papers used to prepare the return totaled 146,000
documents, an increase of 27 percent since TRA86.

More systematic evidence is limited but is now becoming
available. Recent estimates by Slemrod and Blumenthal (1993),
based on a survey of "large" corporations, suggest that the typical

Fortune 500 company spends over $2 million per year in the determination of its taxes, an amount that in the aggregate equals $1.1 billion for the Fortune 500 firms and that exceeds 3 percent of total federal and state corporate income tax collections for these firms. According to the survey, the bulk (70 percent) of these compliance costs are due to the federal corporate income tax. As shown in Table 4, on average compliance costs are less than 0.1 percent of sales for these companies, with a marked tendency for costs as a percent of sales to decline with firm size. Statistical analysis suggests that a 10 percent increase in sales (or other measures of firm size) leads to a roughly 5 percent increase in compliance costs, so that costs rise less than proportionately with size. Slemrod and Blumenthal (1993) also estimate that compliance costs per employee range from $1,200 for smaller corporations in their sample (or corporations that are typically larger than most MSB) to $60 for the larger firms, with an average cost per employee of $125. Average firm compliance costs tended to be lower in the retail and wholesale trade sectors, while businesses in the oil/gas and mining sectors have significantly higher average costs. The survey respondents indicated that the main sources of compliance costs were depreciation provisions and the AMT.

Table 4. Compliance Cost of the Corporate Income Tax
(Dollar amounts in thousands of dollars)

Sales[a]	Personnel Expenditure	Non-personnel Expenditure	Outside Assistance	Total Cost	Total Cost as Percent of Sales
Under $250	312.1	267.0	122.4	701.5	0.47
$250-500	297.9	125.8	94.4	518.1	0.13
$500-750	412.5	176.1	135.8	724.4	0.12
$750-1,250	436.6	153.6	130.0	720.2	0.07
$1,250-2,000	729.4	276.3	182.1	1,187.9	0.08
$2,000-3,000	900.3	642.4	258.0	1,800.6	0.07
$3,000-5,000	1,437.1	611.2	494.2	2,542.4	0.07
$5,000-10,000	2,078.8	741.3	482.6	3,302.7	0.05
Above $10,000	3,966.6	3,963.4	1,096.0	9,025.9	0.05
Average	921.3	494.4	261.6	1,677.3	0.06

Note: [a]Sales are in millions of dollars.

Source: Slemrod and Blumenthal (1993).

Although these results are based on a survey of large corporations, the finding that compliance costs decline with firm size implies that costs for MSB are likely to be well in excess of 0.5 percent of sales. They also suggest that per employee compliance costs for MSB are likely to exceed $1,500 for MSB, and that compliance costs are greater than 1 percent of the value of MSB assets.

Others have calculated different, and generally higher, firm and aggregate compliance costs. Hall (1993) uses information from a survey conducted by Arthur D. Little, Inc. to estimate the total cost of tax compliance for all American businesses at $123 billion in 1993. His figures indicate that compliance costs as a percent of business sales are 0.5 percent for firms with annual sales under $100 million and then fall to roughly 0.1 percent of sales for firms with annual sales in excess of $250 million, with a noticeable tendency for the percentage to fall still more as firm size increases further. Payne (1993) estimates even higher compliance costs. Evidence for other countries suggests that the American experience is a shared one. Studies of the United Kingdom, Australia, and Canada suggest that compliance costs can range from 2 to 24 percent of revenues for selected taxes.

Now it should be remembered that there are some compelling reasons for a complex—and therefore costly—tax system. It would be possible to collect taxes by the imposition of identical taxes on all individuals and on all firms. Such a tax would be quite simple and inexpensive to collect. However, we as a nation have made the collective decision that such a tax system would be an inequitable method of taxation. Once we decide to impose taxes on a tax base that considers individual and firm differences in economic status or performance, complications necessarily emerge. These complications are a price that must be paid for a more equitable tax system.

A related point is that we have often decided to impose taxes with graduated rates, again largely on equity grounds. The use of multiple rates in and of itself does not create any real complexity. However, multiple rates generate incentives for income-shifting across the rate brackets, which increases compliance costs. Multiple rates also make it more difficult for the tax administration to collect taxes because multiple rates make it necessary to distinguish and to identify alternative flows of income.

We have also decided as a nation that the tax system is a suitable mechanism for encouraging activities that are deemed desirable in some sense, as well as for discouraging activities that are unacceptable. The introduction of these provisions clearly complicates the calculation and the administration of taxes.

One form of complexity, however, imposes needless and significant costs on the economy: the complexity that arises from frequent changes in the tax code. Since the Internal Revenue Act of 1954, there have been significant changes in the tax laws on over 30 occasions. These changes obviously add to the complexity of the tax code. These changes—indeed, even the discussion of possible changes—also create uncertainty in the minds of taxpayers, and thereby disrupt their economic decisions. Although it is difficult to measure precisely the magnitude of the resulting economic costs, Skinner (1988) estimates that unstable tax laws cost the economy roughly 0.4 percent of national income every year. My own research (Alm, 1988) also suggests that the behavioral responses to uncertain tax policies can be significant.

Distortions in Business Behavior

Another problem with the existing corporate income tax is that it distorts the decisions of businesses in numerous and inefficient ways. The tax affects the investment and labor choices of corporations, it creates incentives to finance investment with debt rather than equity, it leads firms to keep profits within the corporation rather than pay dividends to owners, it influences mergers and acquisitions of corporations, it affects corporate decisions on inventory valuation, and it changes corporate decisions on tax-deductible activities. Given the potential for enormous tax savings with the introduction of special tax provisions, there are also incentives for businesses to spend money to influence the legislative process. Some of these special provisions have been discussed already, and they create large winners and losers in the corporate income tax.

The actual magnitudes of corporate behavioral responses are in fact highly uncertain, despite numerous attempts to identify and to quantify them.[5] However, there is little doubt that taxes matter in significant ways for corporate decisions, even though the precise way in which they matter is unresolved. This issue is discussed in more detail later.

Saving and Capital Formation

Perhaps the most serious problem with the existing income tax is its effects on saving and capital formation. Under the income tax, the income earned on corporate capital is taxed twice: once when the income is taxed at the corporate level by the corporate income tax, and again at the individual level by the individual income tax when the income is paid out to individuals. Similarly, there is double taxation on individual income, when it is earned as wages and when any interest income is received. Such double taxation clearly reduces the return to saving and investment, thereby lowering economic growth. Put differently, the current income tax penalizes savings and encourages consumption. There is in fact abundant evidence that the saving rate in the United States is relatively low and declining. It is in part because of concern that the American economy consumes too much and saves too little that nearly all proposals for fundamental tax reform seek to replace the income tax with some form of consumption tax.

These (and other) considerations have led to increasing calls for reform of the income tax. Reform must consider changes in the rate and/or the base of the tax. Let me start with rate issues.

B.   The Rate Structure

The argument for lower tax rates is easily stated. Taxes reduce the returns from working, saving, and investing. A reduction in marginal tax rates correspondingly increases these returns, leading to improved incentives to undertake these activities.

Among economists there is almost universal agreement that, at least in theory, individual and business behavior should respond productively and positively to a reduction in marginal tax rates (although even in theory it is possible to get some perverse behavioral responses). In particular, a reduction in marginal tax rates on businesses will certainly lead them to invest more, to hire more workers, to produce more goods and services, to reduce tax avoidance activities, and the like, because the returns to these activities are changed by a reduction in taxation.

However, it is in the area of the magnitude of these responses where there is enormous disagreement. Despite the best efforts of economists to measure these responses, especially for individuals, estimates of behavioral responses are quite varied. It is not possible to predict with much certainty the magnitude of individual or business responses to any given tax rate change.

Now this ambiguity does not mean that taxes do not matter. On the contrary, I believe that there is little doubt that taxes do in fact matter, and matter significantly, in many business decisions. For example, the changes in individual versus corporate taxation in TRA86 are widely viewed as the engine behind the doubling in the number of S corporations and the decline in the number of C corporations (and in corporate tax collections from these firms) over the last ten years. Similarly, as noted above, the changes in capital gains taxes in TRA86 are credited with the enormous positive and negative changes over the period 1985 to 1987. Also, foreign direct investment in the United States doubled in the last quarter of 1986, as firms hurried to beat a change in tax rules on mergers and acquisitions.

However, the precise way in which taxes matter is critical for tax design. Here there is an emerging, if still controversial, consensus on the behavioral responses to tax rate changes. Slemrod (1992) argues convincingly, I believe, that there is a hierarchy of responses to any change in tax rates. The type of behavior most clearly responsive is the *timing* of transactions (e.g., capital gains realizations, foreign direct investment). Such timing changes can be easily made, even if at some cost. In the second tier of responsiveness are purely financial and accounting responses, in which individuals and firms alter the *taxable form* of a transaction even if the economic substance of the action is the same. Included here are firms switching their organization form from C to S corporate status, individuals switching their debt from non-deductible to deductible forms, or individuals switching their saving from non-tax-preferred to tax-preferred forms, all after TRA86. The actions that are likely to be least responsive to tax changes are the *real decisions* of individuals and firms, or their decisions on working, saving, and investing. Much research on business response to investment incentives in the 1980s now tends to conclude that the tax policy was not a major factor in these decisions.[6]

In any event, most economists believe that a reduction in marginal tax rates would generate a variety of beneficial effects, even if the magnitude of these effects is unknown. The choice of a single, flat rate versus the choice of multiple, progressive rates is of relatively little consequence in this outcome, as long as marginal tax rates decline overall.

C. The Tax Base

Of more importance is the choice of the tax base. A striking— and somewhat unnoticed—feature of virtually all of the major tax reform proposals is that they propose to change the tax base from income to consumption; that is, most reforms intend to tax what is spent rather than what is earned.

There are many ways of taxing consumption. Perhaps the most familiar method, at least in the United States, is the *retail sales tax*. Here the tax base is final retail sales of goods and services. This tax is typically used by state and local governments in the United States.

Another variant on a consumption tax is the *value-added tax* (VAT), which has been widely used in Europe for nearly four decades and now has also been adopted in numerous other countries around the world. Value added is the value that a firm adds during production to materials and services purchased from other firms. It equals the difference between a firm's gross receipts and the costs of all intermediate inputs (including the cost of capital goods but excluding wages) used to produce the product; it also equals the sum of wages, interest, rents, and profits of the firm. A tax on the value added of all businesses therefore has as its base the total value of all final products, thereby making a VAT equivalent to national retail sales tax.

Both the retail sales tax and the VAT are collected by and from businesses. A third variant is to tax consumption entirely at the individual level. This *personal consumption tax* is based on the identity that income equals consumption plus saving, so that consumption can be measured as income less saving. An individual's personal consumption could be measured by subtracting amounts saved in allowable assets from all amounts earned (including the returns on and withdrawals from saving). Because the tax is imposed at the individual level, various exemptions and deductions can be allowed, and a graduated tax rate structure can also be introduced. Both features make the tax more progressive. The USA Tax introduced in Congress by Senator Sam Nunn (D-Georgia) and Senator Pete Dominici (R-New Mexico) is a personal consumption tax.

A fourth variant on a consumption tax splits the collection of the tax between businesses and individuals. It is this variant that has been suggested by Hall and Rabushka (1995), that has been introduced in Congress by Representative Dick Armey (R-Texas) and Senator Richard Shelby (R-Alabama), and that was the centerpiece of the Forbes presidential campaign. This tax has been called the *flat tax*.

Recall that the tax base for the VAT is the difference between a firm's gross receipts and the costs of all intermediate inputs (including the cost of capital goods but excluding wages), and so the VAT base equals the sum of wages, interest, rents, and profits of the firm. Suppose that wages are taken out of the tax base at the business level, by allowing them as a business deduction, but that wages are then taxed at the individual level. The total tax base on businesses and individuals is still consumption, but the collection of the tax is now done both at the business and at the individual level. The "Business Tax" in the flat tax is similar to a VAT, except that labor costs are allowed, along with other input costs and capital costs, as a deduction. The "Individual Wage Tax" in the flat tax is imposed on wage income, at the same rate as the business tax; however, because the collection of this part of the tax is at the individual level, some progressivity can be introduced in the flat tax by the use of generous personal allowances.[7]

All major tax reform proposals therefore are quite similar in the choice of a tax base. This similarity allows a brief discussion of their collective advantages and disadvantages, both at a general level and at a level that relates to MSB. Let me begin with the general discussion.

There are at least two major advantages of any consumption tax. First, because a consumption tax removes investment and saving from the tax base, it will lower the cost of capital and/or raise the return on saving. In both cases, the likely responses will be an increase in saving and investment as the intertemporal distortions are removed. Second, because a consumption tax removes capital income from the tax base, it will lower the administrative and compliance costs of taxation. Most of the complexity of the income tax stems from efforts to define, measure, and tax capital income; the measurement of depreciation allowances in particular introduces enormous complexities in the tax code. Because a consumption tax does not tax capital income, these difficulties are eliminated, an especially important advantage in an inflationary environment.

Consumption tax advocates also sometimes argue that a consumption tax would be more equitable than an income tax. Two reasons are cited in support. First, following Thomas Hobbes, they argue that it is more equitable to tax an individual on what he or she takes out of the common pool than what he or she contributes to it. Second, they argue that an equitable tax should treat individuals with equal incomes equally, but this equal treatment should be over the lifetimes of the individuals, not over a single year. Seen in this life-cycle perspective, a consumption tax is an equitable tax because the present values of a flat-rate consumption tax for two individuals with equal incomes (who consume all of their incomes) are the same. In contrast, the present values of an income tax will be different if the pattern of savings differs, because interest income is taxed under an income tax.

The main argument that has been made against any consumption tax is that it will impose a heavier burden on low-income families than on high-income ones. Because the tax base is consumption, and because the fraction of annual income spent on consumption tends to be higher for low-income than for high-income families, a consumption tax is necessarily regressive. Put differently, any consumption (or wage) tax effectively exempts from taxation capital and capital income, and taxes them only when they are consumed. Such a system will reduce the tax burden on high-income families, while increasing the burden on low-income families. A related point is that a consumption tax will also redistribute tax burdens across generations. Those who are or will soon be retired, whose income is almost entirely consumed, will experience a significant increase in tax liabilities. Note, however, that lifetime income may be more relevant than annual income in calculating the average tax rate by income class. There is some evidence that consumption as a proportion of lifetime income is roughly the same at all income levels, which would make even a retail sales tax or a VAT more or less proportional.

The relevant trade-off between consumption versus income taxation is therefore simply stated: are the benefits of improved economic efficiency and greater simplicity worth the costs of the reallocation of tax burdens that consumption taxation will generate?

Consider now the ways in which MSB are likely to be affected by a consumption tax. To make the discussion more concrete, I focus on the effects of a flat tax on MSB. Many, though not all, of these effects would be generated by the other consumption tax reform proposals because many of the tax provisions of these proposals, at least as they relate to businesses, are quite similar. As summarized in Table 5, the various consumption taxes entail largely comparable tax treatment of noncorporate businesses, interest income and expense, deductibility of wages and fringe benefits, expensing of capital purchases, the treatment of foreign-source income, special tax provisions, and the alternative minimum tax.

Compliance Costs

There is widespread agreement that a flat tax would lower compliance costs. However, estimates of the magnitude of the simplification potential of a flat tax vary considerably. Hall (1995)

Table 5.   Some Business Tax Features of Consumption Tax Proposals

Issue	Existing Corporate Income Tax	Armey-Shelby Flat Tax	Nunn-Domenici USA Tax	Value-Added Tax	National Retail Sales Tax
Noncorporate Business Taxed?	No	Yes	Yes	Yes	Yes
Interest Income Taxable?	Yes	No	No	No	No
Interest Expense Deductible?	Yes	No	No	No	No
Wages Deductible?	Yes	Yes	No	No	No
Fringe Benefits Deductible?	Yes	No	No	No	No
Taxes Deductible?	Yes	No	No	No	No
Expensing of Capital?	No	Yes	Yes	Yes	Yes
Tax Foreign-source Income?	Yes	No	No	No	No
Special Tax Credits?	Yes	No	No	No	No
Alternative Minimum Tax?	Yes	No	No	No	No

estimates that the compliance cost of the entire federal income tax system would fall from $140 billion to $8 billion under the flat tax; the compliance costs of other consumption taxes would also be dramatically lower than the current income tax. Some other estimates are considerably smaller.

Now there is little question that the compliance costs for MSB would decline. A major contributor to firm compliance costs is depreciation provisions, especially during inflation, and with a flat tax all capital purchases are immediately expensed. However, it is somewhat misleading to argue that a one-page business tax return (see Table 6 for a standard form) necessarily reduces compliance costs. After all, accounting records will still be needed to fill in the various items on the postcard return. As argued by Hoven (1995) and Feld (1995), these requirements under the flat tax will sometimes be more burdensome than under the existing corporate income tax. The lines between taxable and non-taxable "gross revenue from sales," and between "allowable costs" and non-allowable costs, may be clear in theory, but in practice the distinction will require detailed rules and strict enforcement. For example, what inputs will count as business inputs? How will any personal consumption component of business purchases be determined?

Table 6.   Items on Sample 1995 Business Tax Form for the Flat Tax

1.	Gross Revenue from Sales	1. _____
2.	Allowable Costs (a) Purchases of Goods, Services, and Materials (b) Wages, Salaries, and Pensions (c) Purchases of Capital Equipment, Structures, and Land	 2(a). _____ 2(b). _____ 2(c). _____
3.	Total Allowable Costs (sum of lines 2(a), 2(b), and 2(c))	3. _____
4.	Taxable Income (line 1 less line 3)	4. _____
5.	Tax (19% of line 4)	5. _____
6.	Carry-forward from 1995	6. _____
7.	Interest on Carry-forward	7. _____
8.	Carry-forward into 1996 (line 6 plus line 7)	8. _____
9.	Tax Due (line 5 less line 8, if positive)	9. _____
10.	Carry-forward to 1996 (line 8 less line 5, if positive)	10. _____

Source: Hall and Rabushka (1995).

What inputs will be considered intangibles? What is the distinction between business and personal assets? What types of businesses must file a tax return? How will international transactions, especially those with other countries that maintain a classical corporate income tax, be treated? What is the distinction between active and passive income? These and many other questions will require detailed and complex rules, and these guidelines remain to be specified. There are also other factors that would also act to increase compliance costs. For example, the number of businesses subject to the tax would increase enormously. In short, a consumption tax would almost certainly lower the compliance costs for MSB, but it is easy to overstate the magnitude of the reduction.

Distortions in Business Behavior

It is often claimed that a flat tax would give incentives for firms to base their decisions on the underlying and fundamental benefits and costs of their actions, rather than on the tax benefits and tax costs of the actions. There is considerable appeal to this claim, particularly if the flat tax is introduced at lower tax rates than the current income tax.

However, the tax would not eliminate the tax avoidance games that businesses routinely play. These games relate mainly to items that are classified as "allowable costs" under the flat tax. As one example, firms could avoid taxes by buying inventories at the end of the year. As another example, entrepreneurs could shelter business income by various kinds of investments. As a last example, a flat tax would encourage outsourcing of many activities (the costs of which are allowable costs), rather than hiring more workers (the costs of which are not allowable costs). These and other examples illustrate that the potential for tax avoidance games would still exist. Indeed, a flat tax would almost certainly increase the incentives to find schemes that convert ordinary income to capital income.

Saving and Capital Formation

There is little doubt that expensing of capital purchases would generate an immediate and possibly dramatic increase in investment, and this would increase the rate of economic growth. There would also be winners and losers from the surge in capital formation. Fast-growing, capital-intensive sectors would clearly gain because capital purchases would be deductible; included here are firms in the transportation, utilities, chemical, industrial equipment, paper, tobacco, and communication sectors, as well as start-up companies in any sector. The flat tax treatment of employee compensation, pensions, fringe benefits, exports, and imports also suggests that the textiles, paper, chemical, automobile, and electronics sectors would experience a decline in tax liabilities.

However, it is equally clear that there would also be losers. Businesses that are highly leveraged would lose because interest on debt would not be deductible. Businesses with unused depreciation and depletion allowances would also lose, depending on the transition treatment of the unused allowances; the amounts of these unused provisions are currently estimated at $3 trillion. Partnerships and S corporations would likely lose because they would have to become taxpaying entities. Labor-intensive firms would lose because of the expensing of capital inputs, the elimination of deductibility of the employer's share of social security contributions, and the elimination of deductibility of employee fringe benefits; the service sector and the retail/ wholesale trade sector would lose because they are generally labor-intensive. Businesses that receive large tax benefits from the current tax system would lose (e.g., timber and mining).

There are also other issues. The increase in industrial investment would not be spread evenly across business sectors; again, fast-growing firms in any sector would clearly experience greater increases in investment. The increase in overall investment would almost certainly come at the expense of housing investment. Although a reduction in the stock of housing capital may well be efficiency-enhancing for the economy as a whole, it would also impose costs on those sectors that depend on housing. Expensing of capital purchases might also make business tax revenues countercylical, thereby contributing to aggregate economic instability and discouraging capital formation.

One of the major benefits of a flat tax is greater economic growth. However, the impact of increased saving and capital formation on economic growth is unknown. Hall and Rabushka (1995, p. 87) speculate that "it seems reasonable to predict a 2 to 4 percent increase in GDP on account of added capital formation within seven years." Forbes argues that the growth rate of the economy will double to 5 percent a year. However, other economists suggest that the growth impact is far more uncertain and may in fact be negligible. Endogenous growth models give wildly different predictions about the impact of a consumption tax on economic growth, although the emerging view is that the growth effects would be positive and small (Stokey & Rebelo, 1995).

In sum, the introduction of a flat tax offers the potential for significant benefits. However, these benefits remain highly uncertain. The main benefits relate to increased economic growth and reduced compliance costs. There is simply no way of knowing these magnitudes, and previous predictions of the growth effects of fiscal policies have often been quite inaccurate. No nation has ever introduced such a tax, so there is no historical experience upon which to base predictions. Of course, at least some of the costs of a flat tax are equally uncertain. In particular, if economic growth materializes, then the distributional concerns surrounding a consumption tax will be reduced. Moreover, there is a fear that a flat tax, at least in the form suggested by Forbes, would reduce tax revenues by nearly $200 billion, but this forecast is uncertain and could prove inaccurate if economic growth approaches the more optimistic predictions. Perhaps most significantly—and most unquestionably—the transition problems in moving from the existing income tax to a flat tax are formidable even if manageable (Bradford, 1995; Sarkar & Zodrow, 1993). By necessity, the tax system would have to maintain both the income and the flat tax systems for some period of time, and the costs of such parallel tax systems should not be underestimated.

VI.   CONCLUSIONS: HOW SHOULD MID-SIZE BUSINESS BE TAXED?

So what form has federal government tax policy toward mid-size business taken in the past? Perhaps more importantly, what form should tax policy toward MSB take? There is a widespread consensus that the federal budget should move toward fiscal balance, a consensus with which I agree, so I will not discuss further the continuing efforts to balance the budget. However, both piecemeal tax changes and fundamental tax reforms raise a number of important questions about the tax treatment of MSB. Should MSB receive favorable treatment, at least more favorable treatment than small or large businesses? Should some subsectors within the larger MSB sector be tax-favored? Should MSB be treated the same as firms of different sizes in other sectors of the economy? Indeed, should MSB be treated perhaps less favorably than firms of other sizes?

The answers to these latter, normative questions depend largely upon the answer to a more fundamental question: what goals do we as a society want our tax system to achieve? I believe that a careful examination suggests that the appropriate tax policy involves tradeoffs among essentially three main criteria (Alm, 1996):

- How does the choice of taxes affect the yield of the tax collections, where the yield is defined broadly in terms of the gross collections in excess of administrative and enforcement costs (*adequacy*)?
- How does the choice affect the distribution of the burden of taxation on individuals, where the burden is defined broadly in terms of the tax burden, the compliance cost burden, and the noncompliance cost burden on taxpayers (*equity*)?
- How does the choice affect the decisions of individuals and firms, where the decisions are defined broadly in terms of the responses of the agents to the entire system of fiscal incentives and where the decisions relate also to their effects on economic growth (*efficiency*)?

(Note that I do not define a separate criterion for *simplicity*. Instead, simplicity is implicitly assumed to be considered in its effects on the other three dimensions of a desirable tax system.) Consequently, analysis of taxation requires balancing the tradeoffs between adequacy, equity, and efficiency, where each is broadly defined and commonly measured. What would be the form of the tax rules that would emerge from such a balancing of these conflicting goals?[8]

On equity grounds, taxes are commonly judged by the way in which they achieve the goals of horizontal and vertical equity. Horizontal equity is taken to mean that those who have equal ability-to-pay should pay equal amounts of taxes; vertical equity means that those with greater ability should pay greater taxes. When applied to firms, not individuals, one interpretation of these equity notions is that MSB should pay more in taxes than smaller-sized ones (because the ability-to-pay of MSB is likely to be greater), but they should also pay less in taxes than larger-sized firms. These notions also suggest that MSB firms in different sectors should pay the same taxes.

However, the standard notions of equity lose much of their appeal when applied to firms rather than individuals. If firms of different sizes are treated differently by the tax code, then such treatment necessarily means that the tax treatment of individuals will not satisfy the notions of horizontal and vertical equity. After all, we are ultimately concerned with the distribution of income (and taxes) across individuals, and it is only the individual, not the corporation, who can pay a tax.

It is easier to make the case for preferential, or at least differential, treatment of MSB on efficiency grounds. Suppose, for example, that MSB create beneficial spillovers for society, perhaps in the form of technological advances, job creation, product innovation, or even national defense, all of which are generated more rapidly in firms of medium size than in firms of smaller or larger size. Suppose further that MSB are more likely to face limitations on their abilities to borrow money in the capital market than firms of different size. Suppose finally that the risk of business failure for MSB is greater than for other firms. These arguments can be marshalled to justify the use of taxes either to encourage more MSB activities or to offset the market imperfections that unduly penalize such enterprises.

As with the equity arguments for favorable treatment of MSB, however, these efficiency arguments are considerably more ambiguous. There is little indication that positive spillovers from MSB either are present or are different in size from those of other businesses. Similarly, although there is some data that small firms sometimes face capital market constraints, there is little systematic evidence that similar constraints affect MSB. As discussed at length earlier in the context of capital gains taxation, the positive economic effects of greater entrepreneurial risk-taking, and the ability of the tax system to encourage such risks, is far from clear.

Indeed, there are, I believe, good reasons for uniform treatment of firms of all sizes. A standard result from a branch of economics known as "optimal tax theory" is that a government seeking to balance the goals of adequacy, equity, and efficiency should avoid taxes that distort a firm's choices of inputs or outputs; that is, to the extent possible, taxes should be neutral in their impacts on firm (and individual) decisions. Further, favorable tax treatment of MSB necessarily implies unfavorable tax treatment of other size firms. Finally, it is far from clear that the tax system can be systematically, predictably, and efficiently manipulated to encourage or discourage the specific actions of businesses of any size, despite the almost incessant efforts of government to do so. Unless there are compelling reasons for such favorable treatment—and the discussion above suggests that these arguments are weak—then firms of all sizes should be treated similarly by the tax system. Perhaps it is this type of equal treatment of firms that is best able to balance the goals of adequacy, equity, and efficiency.

In total, these thoughts lead me to suggest the following general rule for the appropriate fiscal policy toward MSB:

> Taxes should be imposed on businesses of all sizes at constant marginal tax rates on a broadly defined consumption tax base, with minimal use of special tax incentives.

What are the reasons for this policy? Constant marginal tax rates reduce compliance costs by reducing the incentive to engage in tax shifting schemes; for related reasons, they reduce administrative costs. Broadly defined tax bases allow lower marginal tax rates to generate a given level of revenue, and so they reduce the distorting effects of taxes on behavior. The use of consumption as a tax base, while perhaps having distributional effects that are controversial and transitional problems that are costly, achieves significant efficiency gains by encouraging saving and investment, reducing tax distortions, and simplifying tax administration and compliance. Tax incentives increase the range of taxpayer and tax agency costs with uncertain impacts on their desired ends, MSB are unlikely to be able to lobby effectively (or more effectively than small or large businesses) for special tax provisions, and, given the extreme diversity in MSB, it is unlikely that a single tax policy can be found behind which all MSB could unite.

My main reason for hesitation lies in the choice of consumption versus income taxation. There are strong grounds for some form of a broad-based income tax, as well as important concerns surrounding any consumption tax, and I find many of these arguments quite persuasive. It would also be possible to achieve many of the goals of consumption taxation by modifying the existing income tax through enhanced tax preferences for saving, increased tax breaks for investment, and the like. However, such changes within the framework of the income tax would not achieve one of the main advantages of a consumption tax: simplification of tax administration and tax compliance. Consequently, I think at this time that it may be more prudent to achieve many of the goals of consumption taxation by in fact moving to a consumption tax, rather than by tinkering with the existing income tax, even though the choice of a consumption tax presents some difficult transition problems.

In short, the tax code should neither encourage or discourage the activities of MSB. Also, it should be designed to eliminate those features that create incentives to engage in tax-advantaged timing or taxable form, as opposed to real, responses. Instead, I believe that the goal of a simple tax that maintains a level-playing field for businesses of all sizes and that encourages saving over consumption is one that we should continue to pursue, even if it is ultimately unattainable.

NOTES

1. See Weidenbaum (1996) for an analysis of the effects of regulatory reforms on MSB, and Macey (1996) for discussion of litigation reforms and MSB.

2. These provisions are examined in detail in Congressional Budget Office (1995a), which also estimates the amount of government spending programs and the magnitude of loans and loan guarantees that promote business and commerce. For a similar study, see Moore and Stamsel (1995).

3. See Smith (1996) for a discussion of federal budget policy.

4. For a detailed discussion of many of these issues, see Barro (1989), Bernheim (1989), Eisner (1989), and Seater (1993).

5. Some of these behavioral responses are discussed in Aaron and Pechman (1981) and Slemrod (1991).

6. For a review of much of this evidence, see Slemrod (1991). However, for more recent evidence that tax reforms had a significant impact on investment, see Cummins, Hassett, and Hubbard (1995).

7. These variants do not exhaust the possible candidates for consumption-like taxes. Another variant (a *wage tax*) relies on the notion that over one's lifetime an individual consumes all of his or her income (in the absence of inheritances or bequests). A tax on consumption is therefore equivalent to a tax on wage income only. Still another variant suggested by McLure and

Zodrow (1996) combines some features of the personal consumption tax with those of the flat tax; they call this consumption tax a *hybrid tax*.

8. Holtz-Eakin (1995) examines similar issues in the context of the tax treatment of small businesses.

REFERENCES

Aaron, H.J., & Pechman, J.A. (Eds.). (1981). *How taxes affect economic behavior*. Washington, DC: The Brookings Institution.

Alm, J. (1988). Uncertain tax policies, individual behavior, and welfare. *The American Economic Review, 78*(1), 237-245.

Alm, J. (1996). What is an 'optimal' tax system? *National Tax Journal, 49*(2), 216-233.

Ball, L., & Mankiw, G. (1995, August/September). Real and financial consequences of budget deficits and debt. In *Budget Deficits and Debt: Issues and Options* (pp. 95-119). Federal Reserve Bank of Kansas City Symposium on Budget Deficits and Debt.

Barro, R.J. (1989). The Ricardian approach to budget deficits. *Journal of Economic Perspectives, 3*(2), 37-54.

Bernheim, B.D. (1989). A neoclassical perspective on budget deficits. *Journal of Economic Perspectives, 3*(2), 55-72.

Bradford, D. (1995). *Consumption taxes: Some fundamental transition issues* (Working Paper 5290). Cambridge, MA: National Bureau of Economic Research.

Budget of the United States Government, fiscal year 1997. (1996). Washington, DC: U.S. Government Printing Office.

Burman, L., & Randolph, W. (1994). Measuring permanent responses to capital-gains tax changes in panel data. *The American Economic Review, 84*(4), 794-809.

Congressional Budget Office. (1995a). *Federal financial support of business*. Washington, DC: Congress of the United States.

Congressional Budget Office (1995b). *The budget outlook*. Washington, DC: Congress of the United States.

Cummins, J.G., Hassett, K.A., & Hubbard, R.G. (1995). *Tax reforms and investment: A cross-country comparison* (Working Paper 5232). Cambridge, MA: National Bureau of Economic Research.

Eisner, R. (1989). Budget deficits: Rhetoric and reality. *Journal of Economic Perspectives, 3*(2), 73-93.

Feld, A.L. (1995). Living with the flat tax. *National Tax Journal, 48*(4), 603-617.

Feldstein, M., Slemrod, J., & Yitzhaki, S. (1980). The effects of taxation on the selling of corporate stock and the realization of capital gains. *Quarterly Journal of Economics, 94*(4), 777-791.

Friedman, B.M. (1993). Learning from the Reagan deficits. *The American Economic Review Papers and Proceedings, 82*(2), 299-304.

Hall, II, A.P. (1993). The high cost of tax compliance for U.S. business. *Tax Foundation Special Report.* Washington, DC: Tax Foundation.

Hall, II, A.P. (1995, June). Alternative tax plans would cut compliance costs. *Tax Features, 39*(5), 1, 3.

Hall, R.E., & Rabushka, A. (1995). *The flat tax* (2nd Ed.). Stanford, CA: Hoover Institution Press.

Holtz-Eakin, D. (1995). Should small businesses be tax-favored? *National Tax Journal, 48*(3), 387-395.

Hoven, V. (1995, August). Flat tax as seen by a tax preparer. *Tax Notes,* 747-755.

Hulten, C., & Schwab, R.M. (1991). *Is there too little public capital?* Washington, DC: American Enterprise Institute.

Internal Revenue Service. (1995, Summer). Corporation income tax returns, 1992. *SOI Bulletin, 15*(1), 7-25.

Kotlikoff, L.J., & Summers, L.H. (1987). Tax incidence. In A.J. Auerbach & M.S. Feldstein (Eds.), *Handbook of public economics volume 2* (pp. 1043-1092). New York: Elsevier Science Publishing Company, Inc.

Macey, J.R. (1996). *Mid-size business, rule-making theory, and litigation reform: Beware of congressmen bearing gifts.* In G.D. Libecap (Ed.), *Advances in the study of entrepreneurship, innovation, and economic growth* (Vol. 8). Greenwich, CT: JAI Press.

McLure, Jr., C.E., & Zodrow, G.R. (1996). A hybrid approach to the direct taxation of consumption. In M.J. Boskin (Ed.), *Handbook of tax reform.* Stanford, CA: Hoover Institution Press.

Moore, S., & Stamsel, D. (1995). *Ending corporate welfare as we know it.* Washington, DC: Cato Institute.

Payne, J.L. (1993). *Costly returns: The burden of the U.S. tax system.* San Francisco, CA: Institute for Contemporary Studies Press.

Sarkar, S., & Zodrow, G.R. (1993). Transitional issues in moving to a direct consumption tax. *National Tax Journal, 46*(3), 359-376.

Seater, J.J. (1993). Ricardian equivalence. *Journal of Economic Literature, 31*(1), 142-190.

Skinner, J. (1988). The welfare cost of uncertain tax policy. *Journal of Public Economics, 34*(2), 129-145.

Slemrod, J. (Ed.). (1991). *Do taxes matter? The impact of the tax reform act of 1986.* Cambridge, MA: The MIT Press.

Slemrod, J. (1992). Do taxes matter? *The American Economic Review Papers and Proceedings.*

Slemrod, J., & Blumenthal, M. (1993). *The income tax compliance cost of big business* (Working Paper No. 93-11) Ann Arbor, MI: The University of Michigan Press.

Smith, J.F. (1996). *An analysis of the potential impacts of federal government budgetary restraints on mid-size business firms in the United States.* In

G.D. Libecap (Ed.), *Advances in the study of entrepreneurship, innovation, and economic growth* (Vol. 8). Greenwich, CT: JAI Press.

Stokey, N.L., & Rebelo, S. (1995). Growth effects of flat-rate taxes. *Journal of Political Economy, 103*(2), 419-450.

Weidenbaum, M. (1996). *The overlooked middle: Government regulation and medium-size business.* In G.D. Libecap (Ed.), *Advances in the study of entrepreneurship, innovation, and economic growth* (Vol. 8). Greenwich, CT: JAI Press.

AN ANALYSIS OF THE POTENTIAL IMPACTS OF FEDERAL GOVERNMENT BUDGETARY RESTRAINTS ON MID-SIZE BUSINESS FIRMS IN THE UNITED STATES

James F. Smith

I. INTRODUCTION

In fiscal year 1995, which ended on September 30 of that year, the government of the United States of America spent $1,514,400,000,000 or a little over $1.5 trillion. Of this enormous spending, $1,225.7 billion was "On-budget" and $288.7 billion was "Off-budget" (Council of Economic Advisers, 1995). Since total revenues were $1,350.6 billion, the deficit was $163.8 billion.

Advances in the Study of Entrepreneurship, Innovation, and Economic Growth,
Volume 8, pages 99-132.
Copyright © 1996 by JAI Press Inc.
All rights of reproduction in any form reserved.
ISBN: 0-7623-0185-6

While most people would condemn that result, since it would have long ago resulted in bankruptcy for any business firm or individual, the fact is, that it is the lowest deficit since fiscal year 1989 and is the smallest in relation to the size of the economy in well over a decade. The size of our federal government deficit in relation to gross domestic product (GDP), the total value of the final output of all goods and services produced in the United States, is much smaller than that of almost all other developed countries except Luxembourg.

In business firms, budgets are normally prepared well in advance of the period they are expected to cover and are generally detailed enough to cover almost all categories of expenditures. While one might expect such behavior to be followed by our national government, nothing could be further from the truth. Medium-size business firms have a huge stake in smaller government because they receive few, if any, benefits from what is often called "corporate welfare." They are too large to benefit from any of the various "set aside" schemes or the loan guarantees of the Small Business Administration. They are too small to benefit very much from the programs that aid big business. For example, aid from the Export-Import Bank does not go to specific electric; it goes to General Electric.

II. SOME BUDGET HISTORY

During most of our history, the United States of America had no consolidated budget at all. The quick description of the situation would be to say that expenditures were very limited except during periods of war and that most revenues were devoted to repaying the debt that had been run up to fight the wars. Individual government departments had their own expenditure authorizations approved by Congress and most revenues came from tariffs.

Total spending by the federal government was $10.8 million in 1800, $15.9 million in 1825, $39.5 million in 1850, and $63.1 million in 1860, which included a $9.9 million deficit from the Post Office Department (Wildavsky, 1982). These sums seem so small that they would be fairly hard to find in the 1995 budget, even after accounting for all the inflation from then until now. Perhaps because of the growing complexity of the world in the early-twentieth century or perhaps simply because our largest leader ever, President Taft, was in the White House, a consensus developed in 1910 that the United States really ought to have a Budget. The business community was in the forefront of this effort.

The federal government had run deficits in ten of the sixteen fiscal years from 1894-1909 (Ott & Ott, 1965). President Taft appointed a Commission on Economy and Efficiency in 1910. After two years of study, the Report of this group strongly urged the establishment of a federal budget system, a proposal endorsed by Taft. After more studies, the usual interminable Congressional hearings, World War I, and eight years of President Wilson, the Congress passed the Budget and Accounting Act of 1921. President Harding signed it into law.

This legislation created the Bureau of the Budget, which has now been changed into the Office of Management and Budget (OMB), and the General Accounting Office as well. This is still the basic law under which the budget is prepared. Of course, in accordance with the Law of Unintended Consequences, the budget has become much less stable, deficits have exceeded the most outrageous forecasts that anyone could have dreamed up in the 1920s, and the activities covered by the budget have become a smaller and smaller share of federal government spending since this law was enacted. Eventually, another law was passed to correct some of these problems.

This was the case with the Budget Impoundment and Control Act of 1974. There were a number of reasons for the development and enactment of this legislation. The conventional wisdom is that it was motivated by Congressional fury at President Nixon for failing to spend all the money that had been appropriated by Congress for public works and a few other programs. While it is true that no President from George Washington to Bill Clinton has ever spent a dime that was not appropriated by Congress, it is also true that most Presidents had not spent all the monies appropriated, a process known as "impoundment." The 1974 Act took this power away from the President unless such actions were explicitly approved by the Congress.

The 1974 Act also created the Congressional Budget Office (CBO) to give Congress its own set of budget experts to deal with those in the Administration. The Act also shifted the fiscal year from one that ended on June 30 to the current September 30. In terms of attempting to improve the budgeting process, the Act set up a system under which Congress proposed two Budget Resolutions, which for the first time covered all spending by the federal government. The first concurrent resolution is scheduled for adoption by May 15 every year, prior to any votes on appropriations bills. The second resolution is scheduled for September 15, just prior to the start of the new fiscal year.

III.   THE BUDGET PROCESS

When it comes to fiscal policy in the United States, the old saw "The President proposes and Congress disposes" has never been more relevant. Under the law, the President must submit a Budget to the Congress by the first Monday in February. These are normally the multivolume sets of documents that some people like to drop on tables to dramatize with a resounding thud the size and complexity of the federal government. During the Bush Administration, OMB Director Richard Darman put out a fourteen-pound one volume budget tome that was somewhat larger than the Manhattan telephone directory, but the Clinton Administration returned to the multivolume precedent of earlier administrations.

In 1996 President Clinton was forced by the most unusual circumstances discussed later in this chapter to submit a budget that was actually just a 25-page outline. This is probably a onetime event and he later submitted the familiar multivolume budget documents. Most of the employees of OMB and large numbers of people in every cabinet department and independent agency spend most of their time every year preparing the next year's budget. A preliminary budget for the following year is sent out to all affected units of the federal government by OMB in October, right after a new fiscal year has begun. The agencies and departments fill out the forms, often after meetings with OMB personnel to seek clarification or to resolve any differences of amounts allocated to particular uses. Any disagreements or disputes that are not resolved in this process are taken up in meetings between the agency or department head and the director of OMB. If there are still areas where agreement has not been reached, then these are resolved in cabinet meetings or by the President himself.

All of this effort is usually completed by late November or early December, so that the comprehensive budget can be prepared for release in early February. A very important concomitant activity is the development of the economic assumptions that will be used in estimating revenues and expenses that are particularly sensitive to economic conditions. This activity is organized by a group known as "the Troika," which is comprised of the Secretary of the Treasury, the Chairman of the President's Council of Economic Advisers (CEA), and the Director of OMB. These officials set the broad policy directives under which the assumptions are actually prepared.

While the Troika is chaired by the Secretary of the Treasury, the actual development of the economic assumptions is delegated to the "T-2," which is chaired by the member of the CEA who is responsible for macroeconomic analysis. The other members of T-2 are the assistant secretary of the Treasury for economic policy and the chief economist of OMB. These officials meet regularly on this topic and develop a range of economic scenarios that are run through various large econometric models of the U.S. economy.

The actual model runs and much of the detailed analyses are done by the so-called "T-3," who are the professional civil servants in the three agencies who have in most cases been doing these types of econometric simulations for many years. Ultimately, the Troika agree on the assumptions and often the President signs off on this in advance of publication.

IV. THE IMPORTANCE OF
THE ECONOMIC ASSUMPTIONS

It should be obvious to even the most casual observer that, if spending and revenue laws do not change, the outcomes will be

Table 1.   Effects on CBO Budget Projections of Selected Changes
In Economic Assumptions (By fiscal year, in billions of dollars)

	1995	1996	1997	1998	1999	2000
Real Growth: Effect of 1-Percentage-Point Lower Annual Rate Beginning January 1995						
Change in Revenues	-9	-27	-49	-72	-97	-125
Change in Outlays						
Net interest (Debt service)	a	2	5	9	15	24
Mandatory Spending	1	3	5	7	10	12
Total	1	4	9	16	25	36
Change in Deficit	10	32	59	88	122	161
Unemployment: Effect of 1-Percentage-Point Higher Annual Rate Beginning January 1995						
Change in Revenues	-35	-51	-54	-56	-58	-61
Change in Outlays						
Net interest (Debt service)	1	5	9	13	17	23
Mandatory spending	3	5	6	6	6	6
Total	4	10	14	19	23	29
Change in Deficit	39	61	68	74	81	89
Inflation: Effect of 1-Percentage-Point Higher Annual Rate Beginning January 1995						
Change in Revenues	7	21	37	54	72	92
Change in Outlays						
Net interest						
Higher rates	5	17	24	29	34	40
Debt service	a	a	a	1	1	2
Discretionary spending	a	a	1	3	9	14
Mandatory spending	3	7	15	25	37	49
Total	8	24	40	58	81	105
Change in Deficit	1	3	3	4	9	13
Interest Rates: Effect of 1-Percentage-Point Higher Annual Rates Beginning January 1995						
Change In Revenues	0	0	0	0	0	0
Change In Outlays						
Net interest						
Higher rates	5	17	24	29	34	40
Debt service	a	1	3	5	7	10
Mandatory spending	2	1	1	1	1	1
Total	8	19	28	35	42	50
Change in Deficit	8	19	28	35	42	50

Note: a. Less than $500 million.

Source: Congressional Budget Office. The Economic and Budget Outlook: Fiscal Years 1996-2000, p. 78.

wildly different in an economy with a ten percent interest rate on long term bonds rather than a five percent rate. Similarly, an economy that is growing at four percent a year in real terms will produce very different outcomes from one that is only growing at two percent a year or from one that is declining. Smaller changes come about from differences in unemployment rates or the rate of inflation.

Every year, CBO publishes updated information on these so-called "rules of thumb" and their impact on the budget. Table 1 shows these results. This table should be carefully reviewed so that there can be no disagreement that anyone who expects budget outcomes to match plans set out by the federal government is bound to be disappointed. The big argument of late 1995 and early 1996 over whether a seven year budget agreement would be scored by CBO or OMB views, which was settled in favor of using the CBO economic scenario (shown later in this chapter), was basically a discussion over alternative economic forecasts and different rules of thumb.

The only way to derive these rules of thumb is to use econometric models. What econometric models do is evaluate how economic interrelationships have worked in the past and use those results to project how the future may look given a particular set of economic assumptions.

Professor Robert E. Lucas, Jr. of the University of Chicago won the Nobel Memorial Prize in Economic Science in 1995 for, among other things, proving mathematically that it is extremely unlikely that forecasts about the future growth of the economy will prove true unless there are no changes in policy. This work, known as the "Lucas critique," has not eliminated the need for long term economic forecasting, but it has caused most business firms to focus on developing alternative scenarios rather than relying on a single point forecast of the economic future.

V. THE NEED FOR A BUDGET POLICY

Throughout the history of the United States, major changes in government spending in relation to the size of the economy have been driven by perceptions that the debt of the federal government was "too high" or "out of control" and needed to be cut back sharply. In his famous book, historian Charles Beard argued that a major reason for the development of the Constitution in 1787 was to provide a mechanism for paying off the Revolutionary War debt run up by the various states as well as by the Continental Congress (Beard, 1935).

While he was not successful in getting assumptions of the debts of the states included in the national debt during the writing of the Constitution, Alexander Hamilton kept lobbying for this while serving as the Secretary of the Treasury in the Washington Administration. He was finally successful when he tied this issue in with those who wanted to move the capital from New York to Washington, D.C. Thus, our nation's capital owes its current location to the assumption of the debts of the states in 1790 (Wildavsky, 1982, p. 49).

These debts were paid down, but then the costs of the War of 1812 ballooned the deficits and thus the level of debt. This led to a general feeling during the Jackson Administration (1829-1836) that the national debt should be eliminated. It was, amazingly enough, and then the great issue became what to do with the surplus. It was initially returned to the states, but they soon protested that they had no productive uses for the money, so taxes were reduced. The Panic of 1837, primarily caused by the revocation of the charter of the Second Bank of the United States in 1836 and the subsequent financial confusion, solved this problem of excessive surpluses. President Polk (1845-1849), famous as the only graduate of the University of North Carolina to become President of the United States and also as the man who brought the Republic of Texas into the United States, restored budget balance. The war years of 1860-1865 and the subsequent costs of Reconstruction led to increases in deficits and the national debt. The Morrill Act of 1862 made land grants to the states to create colleges and universities that are still very important today and the National Bank Act of 1863 moved to change the banking system. The prevailing opinion was still that budgets should be balanced whenever possible.

Nobel laureate James Buchanan of George Mason University has written extensively on the topic that until after World War II, the notion that the federal government should run a deficit for reasons other than coping with either a war or a significant economic downturn was widely considered to be immoral. Buchanan blames John Maynard Keynes and the followers of his theory as espoused in *The General Theory of Employment, Interest, and Money* for the breakdown of this consensus (Buchanan, 1989).

Thus, it might be said that for most of the history of the United States we had a national policy to balance the budget except in periods of economic crisis or war and to run surpluses after such periods. In the period from 1945 to 1975 or so there was probably a consensus that the budget ought to be balanced under conditions of full employment.

This was unfortunately observed far less frequently in practice than in theory. The U.S. economy was at full employment during much of that period. President Truman managed to achieve budget surpluses in four of his seven years in office and President Eisenhower achieved three surpluses in eight years. Since then, the only year with a budget surplus was 1969. That came about because a temporary ten percent income tax surcharge was passed in October, 1968, and made retroactive to the beginning of the year.

Even the world's most creative tax advisor couldn't figure out how to shelter income that had already been earned, so the budget surplus of fiscal year 1969 became a fact. The surplus was $3.2 billion on revenues of $186.9 billion. That was the last budget surplus recorded by the federal government. No one knows when the next one will come, but it probably isn't a good idea to bet on any year before 2005.

From 1792-1930, the federal government ran surpluses in 92 years, including 1921-1929, and had deficits in only 46 years (Ott & Ott, 1965, p. 49). Since 1930, there have been only 10 years with a surplus and 55 deficits have been recorded. Few, if any other, budget analysts have dealt with the area of spending by the federal government longer or more thoughtfully than has Herbert Stein. His outstanding 1989 book, *Governing The $5 Trillion Economy*, which built on the 1947 document "Taxes and the Budget: A Program for Prosperity in a Free Economy" published by the

Committee for Economic Development, built a very convincing case for the development of a national budget policy.

One of Dr. Stein's strongest recommendations is that a President should submit a four year budget early in his term and the Congress should act on the same basis (Stein, 1989, p. 136). He shows that the current practice of year to year budgeting has created a great deal of instability in both the budget and the economy. Dr. Stein argues for a surplus or deficit goal when the economy is running near full employment without any strong actions to correct for temporary deviations. In a well known later article, he pointed out that the American people and the Congress have still not agreed on what the budget policy of the United States ought to be (Stein, 1993, November 29).

VI.   FAILED ATTEMPTS TO BALANCE THE BUDGET

Over the period 1980-1996, there have been five major attempts to reduce the rate of growth of government spending. The lack of success of these efforts can be deduced from the fact that the total spending of the federal government has grown from $590.9 billion in fiscal year 1980 to $1,514.4 billion in fiscal year 1995 while the total gross domestic product (GDP) has only grown from $2,708.0 to $7296.2 billion.

The first effort only applied for one year and was arguably the most successful. This was the effort know as Gramm-Latta 1981 after then Democratic Representative Phil Gramm of Texas and Delbert Latta (R-Ohio), the ranking minority member of the House Budget Committee. They designed a Budget Resolution that turned out to be strong enough to hold down a wide variety of spending options in fiscal year 1982. The combination of the fairly severe 1981-1982 recession and the growing frustration of many members of Congress with their inability to deliver the programs that they had promised to deliver to their constituents meant that this plan could not succeed in subsequent years.

After the failure of a "Budget Summit" meeting at the White House in 1984, Senators Phil Gramm (R-Texas), Warren Rudman

(R-New Hampshire), and Ernest C. "Fritz" Hollings (D-South Carolina) got together and proposed what became the Balanced Budget and Emergency Deficit Control Act of 1985. This legislation, which is much better known as Gramm-Rudman-Hollings or simply "GRH 1" set specific deficit goals for each fiscal year from 1986-1991, with the goal of a balanced budget in 1991. Failure to reach a balanced budget was to be punished by the dreaded "sequestration," which would literally revoke spending authority previously granted by Congress in a draconian manner. One half of the sequestered amounts, which were reductions in planned spending, was to come out of the defense budget, where the President's only discretion would be to exempt the salaries of military personnel or to let those be cut, and the other half would come out of all other spending except for Social Security and interest on the national debt.

It quickly became apparent that the only way the deficit targets set out in GRH 1 would be met was by large sequesters, so Congress did what it usually does in difficult situations and changed the law. The Balanced Budget and Emergency Deficit Control Reaffirmation Act of 1987 set new targets for the deficit with the requirement for a balanced budget now moved to fiscal year 1993.

As shown in Table 2, which compares the deficit goals with the actual results since 1986, it was obvious that a major sequester of over $100 billion was coming in fiscal year 1991. President Bush was not willing to face this in the fall of 1990, especially the prospect of a $50 billion cut in defense spending when "Desert Shield" was in the process of building up to "Desert Storm" in early 1991 to drive Iraqi troops out of Kuwait. Thus, we got the Budget Enforcement Act of 1990, which was Title XIII of the Omnibus Budget Reconciliation Act of 1990.

This law abandoned fixed caps on the size of the deficit in exchange for limits on discretionary spending, a pay-as-you-go process for so-called entitlement spending, and credit reforms. The full law is probably better remembered by most people as the one that proved to them that while they read George Bush's lips as saying "No new taxes," he had really said "Don't nuke Texas."

Table 2. A Comparison of Gramm-Rudman-Hollings
Budget Deficit Requirements With Actual Outcomes:
1984-1994
(Billions)

Fiscal Year	Actual	GRH 1	GRH 2
1984	$185.4	N/A	N/A
1985	212.3	N/A	N/A
1986	221.2	$172	N/A
1987	149.8	144	N/A
1988	155.2	108	$136
1989	152.5	72	100
1990	221.4	36	64
1991	269.2	0	28
1992	290.4	0	0
1993	255.1	0	0
1994	203.2	0	0

Source: ("Economic Indicators" December, 1995, p. 32).

Three years later President Clinton was faced with deficit projections of $200 billion or more "as far as the eye could see." This led to the Omnibus Budget Reconciliation Act of 1993, which attracted no Republican votes in the House of Representatives or the Senate. This law raised income tax rates again and extended the caps on discretionary spending through fiscal year 1998. This was also the law that created the gasoline tax of 4.3 cents a gallon, to be used solely for deficit reduction, that led to the temporary repeal plan in May, 1996.

VII. THE CURRENT EFFORT TO BALANCE THE BUDGET

In the first five months of fiscal year 1996, which began on October 1, 1995, the Congress has passed nine continuing resolutions (CR's) to keep the government going. Of course, there have been several partial shutdowns of the federal government, some because no appropriations legislation had been signed into law and some because of terrible weather in various parts of the country.

Before finally completing the budget on April 26, 1996, the United States operated under 13 different CR's that funded the federal government temporarily. Of the 13 appropriations bills that

Table 3. Economic Projections for Calendar Years 1996 Through 2006 Assuming Current Policy

	Preliminary[a] 1995	Forecast 1996	Forecast 1997	1998	1999	2000	2001	2002	Projected 2003	2004	2005	2006
Nominal GDP (Billions of dollars)	7,248	7,584	7,943	8,324	8,730	9,156	9,603	10,071	10,563	11,078	11,619	12,185
Nominal GDP (Percentage change)	4.6	4.6	4.7	4.8	4.9	4.9	4.9	4.9	4.9	4.9	4.9	4.9
Real GDP[b] (Percentage change)	2.1	2.0	1.9	2.0	2.1	2.1	2.1	2.1	2.1	2.1	2.1	2.1
Chained Price Index (Percentage change)	2.5	2.6	2.8	2.7	2.7	2.7	2.7	2.7	2.7	2.7	2.7	2.7
CPI-U[c] (Percentage change)	2.8	2.8	3.1	3.0	2.9	2.9	2.9	3.0	3.0	3.0	3.0	3.0
Unemployment Rate (Percent)	5.6	5.8	6.0	6.0	6.0	6.0	6.0	6.0	6.0	6.0	6.0	6.0
Three-Month Treasury Bill Rate (Percent)	5.5	4.9	4.8	4.8	4.8	4.8	4.8	4.8	4.8	4.8	4.8	4.8
Ten-Year Treasury Note Rate (Percent)	6.6	6.1	6.4	6.4	6.4	6.4	6.4	6.4	6.4	6.4	6.4	6.4

(continued)

Table 3. (Continued)

	Preliminary[a] 1995	Forecast 1996	1997	1998	1999	2000	Projected 2001	2002	2003	2004	2005	2006
Nominal GDP												
Tax Bases (Billions of Dollars)												
Corporate profit	579	599	612	616	620	629	648	672	703	741	780	822
Other taxable income	1,529	1,595	1,662	1,757	1,859	1,958	2,058	2,157	2,259	2,367	2,482	2,604
Wage and salary disbursements	3,420	3,592	3,760	3,935	4,124	4,322	4,528	4,743	4,969	5,205	5,452	5,711
Total	5,528	5,786	6,035	6,308	6,603	6,909	7,233	7,572	7,931	8,313	8,714	9,137
Tax Bases (Percentage of GDP)												
Corporate profits	8.0	7.9	7.7	7.4	7.1	6.9	6.7	6.7	6.7	6.7	6.7	6.7
Other taxable income	21.1	21.0	20.9	21.1	21.3	21.4	21.4	21.4	21.4	21.4	21.4	21.4
Wage and salary disbursements	47.2	47.4	47.3	47.3	47.2	47.2	47.2	47.1	47.0	47.0	46.9	46.9
Total	76.3	76.3	76.0	75.8	75.6	75.5	75.3	75.2	75.1	75.0	75.0	75.0

Notes: GDP = gross domestic product.

a. Consistent with the first official estimate for 1995 published on March 4, 1996.

b. Based on chained (1992) dollars.

c. CPI-U is the consumer price index for all urban consumers.

Sources: Congressional Budget Office; Department of Commerce, Bureau of Economic Analysis; Department of Labor, Bureau of Labor Statistics; Federal Reserve Board.

112

Table 4. Economic Projections for Calendar Years 1996 Through 2006 Assuming Balanced Budget Policy

	Preliminary[a] 1995	Forecast		Projected								
		1996	1997	1998	1999	2000	2001	2002	2003	2004	2005	2006
Nominal GDP (Billions of dollars)	7,248	7,584	7,946	8,333	8,745	9,177	9,631	10,108	10,608	11,133	11,684	12,261
Nominal GDP (Percentage change)	4.6	4.6	4.8	4.9	4.9	4.9	4.9	4.9	4.9	4.9	4.9	4.9
Real GDP[b] (Percentage change)	2.1	2.0	2.0	2.1	2.2	2.2	2.2	2.2	2.2	2.2	2.2	2.2
Chained Price Index (Percentage change)	2.5	2.6	2.8	2.7	2.7	2.7	2.7	2.7	2.7	2.7	2.7	2.7
CPI-U[c] (Percentage change)	2.8	2.8	3.1	3.0	2.9	2.9	2.9	3.0	3.0	3.0	3.0	3.0
Unemployment Rate (Percent)	5.6	5.8	6.0	6.0	6.0	6.0	6.0	6.0	6.0	6.0	6.0	6.0
Three-Month Treasury Bill Rate (Percent)	5.5	4.9	4.8	4.3	3.9	3.7	3.7	3.7	3.7	3.7	3.7	3.7
Ten-Year Treasury Note Rate (Percent)	6.6	5.7	5.5	5.3	5.3	5.3	5.3	5.3	5.3	5.3	5.3	5.3

(continued)

Table 4. (Continued)

	Preliminary[a] 1995	Forecast					Projected					
		1996	1997	1998	1999	2000	2001	2002	2003	2004	2005	2006
Tax Bases **(Billions of dollars)**												
Corporate profits	579	602	637	668	691	715	741	778	817	857	899	944
Other taxable income	1,529	1,590	1,635	1,700	1,779	1,860	1,946	2,032	2,127	2,227	2,334	2,448
Wage and salary disbursements	3,420	3,592	3,762	3,939	4,131	4,332	4,541	4,761	4,990	5,230	5,482	5,746
Total	5,528	5,784	6,034	6,307	6,601	6,907	7,228	7,570	7,933	8,315	8,715	9,138
Tax Bases **(Percentage of GDP)**												
Corporate profits	8.0	7.9	8.0	8.0	7.9	7.8	7.7	7.7	7.7	7.7	7.7	7.7
Other taxable income	21.1	21.0	20.6	20.4	20.3	20.2	20.1	20.0	20.0	20.0	20.0	20.0
Wage and salary disbursements	47.2	47.4	47.3	47.3	47.2	47.2	47.2	47.1	47.0	47.0	46.9	46.8
Total	76.3	76.3	75.9	75.7	75.5	75.3	75.0	74.9	74.8	74.7	74.6	74.5

Notes: GDP = gross domestic product.

a. Consistent with the first official estimate for 1995 published on March 4, 1996.

b. Based on chained (1992) dollars.

c. CPI-U is the consumer price index for all urban consumers.

Sources: Congressional Budget Office; Department of Commerce, Bureau of Economic Analysis; Department of Labor, Bureau of Labor Statistics; Federal Reserve Board.

make up the so-called "discretionary" part of the budget, only five had been enacted into law by February, 1996. This is why it was so difficult for President Clinton to prepare his proposed 1997 budget on the legally required timetable.

There has been an agreement between Congress and the President to design a budget that is in balance in fiscal year 2002 using the economic assumptions of the CBO. These assumptions are detailed in Tables 3 and 4, as projected by CBO in April, 1996 (Congressional Budget Office, 1996).

A quick glance at the tables will show you that real economic growth is expected to be 2.1 or 2.2 percent a year through 2002, much less than in 1992-1995. Also, the consumer price index is expected to increase by 2.9-3.0 percent a year, much worse than recent performance. Interest rates are expected to maintain a constant relationship to the rate of inflation and thus, not surprisingly, to rise from current levels and remain there.

No one seems to have noticed that there is no recession anywhere in these assumptions. My own forecasts do not have a recession until 2002, but this is deemed to be wildly optimistic by most forecasters. None of this is to cast blame on the people who prepared the CBO assumptions. It is impossible to put together budget assumptions without making economic forecasts. The basic point is that there is a good chance these projections will turn out to be wrong on the pessimistic side, which would turn out to be good news indeed.

Table 5 shows the path to a balanced budget as projected by CBO under the Balanced Budget Act that President Clinton vetoed on December 6, 1995. Note that it required actual cuts in discretionary spending and very strong reductions in the rate of growth of Medicare and Medicaid spending from past trends. Defense spending is already projected to reach its smallest share of GDP since 1940 by the year 2000. The budget plan in Table 6, which should be pretty close to whatever final plan emerges from the negotiations between Congressional leaders and President Clinton, would still result in federal government spending of $1,836.0 billion in fiscal year 2002.

The basic problem is that spending by the federal government has gotten completely out of control in the 1990s. In his very

Table 5. The Path to a Balanced Budget

CBO'S DECEMBER BASELINE PROJECTIONS WITH DISCRETIONARY INFLATION AFTER 1998
(By fiscal year)

	1996	1997	1998	1999	2000	2001	2002	2003	2004	2005
				In Billions of Dollars						
Revenues										
Individual income	628	657	690	727	766	807	853	901	953	1,008
Corporate income	168	179	186	193	200	208	215	223	232	242
Social insurance	506	529	552	579	608	635	666	697	729	766
Other	121	122	124	126	129	133	138	144	150	156
Total	1,423	1,487	1,553	1,625	1,703	1,783	1,871	1,965	2,064	2,172
On-budget	1,056	1,103	1,151	1,202	1,259	1,319	1,385	1,456	1,531	1,611
Off-budget	367	384	402	423	444	464	486	509	533	560
Outlays										
Discretionary[a]	552	554	556	572	589	606	624	643	662	682
Mandatory	881	954	1,007	1,075	1,147	1,215	1,297	1,380	1,473	1,580
Deposit insurance	-8	-4	-3	-2	-2	-2	-1	-1	-1	-1
Net interest	243	249	252	255	256	262	271	282	293	307
Offsetting receipts	-73	-75	-77	-79	-82	-86	-91	-94	-98	-307
Total	1,595	1,668	1,736	1,820	1,907	1,994	2,100	2,209	2,330	2,466
On-budget	1,292	1,354	1,407	1,476	1,548	1,618	1,708	1,800	1,902	2,020
Off-budget	303	315	329	345	359	376	392	409	427	446
Deficit										
Deficit	172	182	183	195	204	211	228	244	266	294
On-budget deficit	236	251	256	273	289	299	323	344	372	408
Off-budget surplus	63	69	73	78	86	88	94	100	106	114
Debt Held by the Public	3,791	3,987	4,184	4,395	4,614	4,841	5,085	5,345	5,627	5,936
Memorandum										
Gross Domestic Product	7,328	7,694	8,075	8,474	8,894	9,334	9,796	10,282	10,793	11,329

(continued)

Table 5. (Continued)

	1996	1997	1998	1999	2000	2001	2002	2003	2004	2005
				As a Percentage of GDP						
Revenues										
Individual income	8.6	8.5	8.5	8.6	8.6	8.6	8.7	8.8	8.8	8.9
Corporate income	2.3	2.3	2.3	2.3	2.2	2.2	2.2	2.2	2.2	2.1
Social insurance	6.9	6.9	6.8	6.8	6.8	6.8	6.8	6.8	6.8	6.8
Other	1.6	1.6	1.5	1.5	1.4	1.4	1.4	1.4	1.4	1.4
Total	19.4	19.3	19.2	19.2	19.1	19.1	19.1	19.1	19.1	19.2
On-budget	14.4	14.3	14.3	14.2	14.2	14.1	14.1	14.2	14.2	14.2
Off-budget	5.0	5.0	5.0	5.0	5.0	5.0	5.0	5.0	4.9	4.9
Outlays										
Discretionary[a]	7.5	7.2	6.9	6.8	6.6	6.5	6.4	6.3	6.1	6.0
Mandatory	12.0	12.3	12.5	12.7	12.9	13.0	13.2	13.4	13.7	13.9
Deposit insurance	-0.1	-0.1	b	b	b	b	b	b	b	b
Net interest	3.3	3.2	3.1	3.0	2.9	2.8	2.8	2.7	2.7	2.7
Offsetting receipts	-1.0	-1.0	-1.0	-0.9	-0.9	-0.9	-0.9	-0.9	-0.9	-0.9
Total	21.8	21.7	21.5	21.5	21.4	21.4	21.4	21.5	21.6	21.8
On-budget	17.6	17.6	17.4	17.4	17.4	17.3	17.4	17.5	17.6	17.8
Off-budget	4.1	4.1	4.1	4.1	4.0	4.0	4.0	4.0	4.0	3.9
Deficit	2.4	2.4	2.3	2.3	2.3	2.3	2.3	2.4	2.5	2.6
On-budget deficit	3.2	3.3	3.2	3.2	3.3	3.2	3.3	3.3	3.4	3.6
Off-budget surplus	0.9	0.9	0.9	0.9	1.0	0.9	1.0	1.0	1.0	1.0
Debt Held by the Public	51.7	51.8	51.8	51.9	51.9	51.9	51.9	52.0	52.1	52.4

(continued)

Table 5. (Continued)

OUTLAYS, REVENUES, AND DEFICITS UNDER THE BALANCED BUDGET ACT, USING CBO'S DECEMBER BASELINE ASSUMPTIONS (By fiscal year, in billions of dollars)

Outlays							
Discretionary	534	524	518	516	520	516	515
Mandatory							
Medicare[a]	193	207	218	229	248	267	289
Medicaid	97	104	109	113	118	122	127
Other	501	526	551	580	610	632	664
Subtotal	791	838	878	922	975	1,021	1,081
Net Interest	243	247	249	247	242	241	240
Total	1,568	1,609	1,644	1,685	1,738	1,779	1,836
Revenues	1,417	1,450	1,518	1,588	1,666	1,745	1,839
Deficit	151	159	127	97	73	34	-3

Notes: a. Projections assume that discretionary spending is equal to the spending limits that are in effect through 1998 and grows at the rate of inflation after that.
b. Less than 0.05 percent.
CBO's estimates of the budgetary effects of the Balanced Budget Act are illustrative because the legislation was not enacted by the November 15, 1995 date assumed by its drafters. Legislative modifications required to reflect a later enactment date would determine the actual budgetary effects of the bill.
c. Includes spending for Medicare benefit payments only; excludes Medicare premium receipts and spending for graduate medical education. Including premiums, net Medicare spending would be $170 billion in 1996, $182 billion in 1997, $190 billion in 1998, $199 billion in 1999, $213 billion in 2000, $228 billion in 2001, and $246 billion in 2002.

Source: Congressional Budget Office (1995).

Table 6. The Fiscal Dividend

CHANGE IN THE DEFICIT RESULTING FROM THE ECONOMIC EFFECTS
OF BALANCING THE BUDGET IN 2002 (By fiscal year, in billions of dollars)

	1996	1997	1998	1999	2000	2001	2002	Total, 1996-2002
Change Resulting from Lower Interest Rates								
Outlays (Net interest)	-1	-8	-16	-26	-34	-38	-40	-162
Revenues[a]								
Federal Reserve earnings	b	1	1	3	4	5	5	20
Shift in income shares	-5	-12	-18	-19	-18	-17	-16	-105
Subtotal	-6	-19	-32	-42	-48	-50	-50	-247
Change Resulting from Higher Gross Domestic Product								
Revenues[b]	-1	-2	-3	-5	-6	-8	-10	-35
Total Effect on the Deficit	-7	-21	-36	-47	-54	-58	-60	-282

Notes: This estimate does not include debt service on the estimated change in the deficit.

a. Revenue reductions are shown as positive because they increase the deficit.

b. Less than $500 million.

Source: Congressional Budget Office (1995).

perceptive monograph *Broken Promises: What's Gone Wrong with The Economy in the 1990s,* Stephen Moore, director of fiscal policy studies at the Cato Institute, points out that for every dollar of peace dividend resulting from the end of the Cold War, Congress has spent $2.75 on domestic programs (Moore, 1996, p. 14). This has resulted in non-defense federal spending at 18.2 percent of GDP in 1995, the highest ever recorded.

Former CEA Chairman Paul McCracken has written:

> A decision to go with budgets that involve deficits is a decision to have a future economy delivering lower incomes. In that sense we are living it up at the expense of our children and grandchildren. The logic is inexorable, and the result is unacceptable. It is doubtful if that is what people want to do (McCracken, 1995, p. 10).

Most reasonable people agree with this statement. This is the primary reason why there is such an effort to reach a budget agreement that would balance the budget by 2002. However, this would only serve as a downpayment on a far bigger problem in subsequent years. In her April 17, 1996, testimony to the House Budget Committee, CBO Director June E. O'Neill laid out the dire potential if major budget changes are not made soon. If there are no changes made in major programs, we could wind up in 2025 with a deficit at 12 percent of GDP and a public debt that was 135 percent of GDP (O'Neill, 1996. p. 20). These results are shown in Table 7. The deficit was only that big during World War II and the debt has never been so large. Furthermore, the debt to GDP ratio would spiral out of control in subsequent years as interest payments became an ever larger part of federal spending. The primary cause of this disastrous scenario is shown in Table 8, which contains projections from the trustees of the Social Security Old Age and Survivors and Disability Insurance (OASDI) Trust Funds that the number of U.S. citizens 65 or older in 2030 will be more than double the number in 1990, while the number of 20-64 year olds will grow only 25 percent.

Table 7. Projections of Federal Receipts and Expenditures Measured by the National Income and Product Accounts Base Scenario Without Economic Feedbacks, Selected Calendar Years (As a percentage of gross domestic product)

	Preliminary 1995[a]	2000	2005	2010	2015	2020	2025	2050
Receipts	20	20	20	20	20	20	20	20
Expenditures								
Federal consumption expenditures	6	6	5	5	5	5	5	5
Transfers, grants, and subsidies								
Social Security	5	5	5	6	5	6	5	7
Medicare	3	3	4	4	6	6	7	8
Medicaid	1	2	2	2	3	3	3	4
Other	5	3	4	4	4	4	4	4
Net interest	<u>3</u>	<u>3</u>	<u>3</u>	<u>3</u>	<u>4</u>	<u>5</u>	<u>7</u>	<u>17</u>
Total	23	22	23	24	27	29	32	45
Deficit	2	3	3	5	7	9	12	25
Debt Held by the Public[c]	51	51	56	62	77	102	135	378

Assume Discretionary Spending Grows with the Economy After 2005[b]

(continued)

121

Table 7. (Continued)

	Preliminary 1995[a]	2000	2005	2010	2015	2020	2025	2050
Receipts	20	20	20	20	20	20	20	20
Assume Discretionary Spending Grows with Inflation After 2005								
Expenditures								
Federal consumption expenditures	6	6	5	5	4	4	4	3
Transfers, grants, and subsidies								
Social Security	5	5	5	6	5	6	6	7
Medicare	3	3	4	4	5	6	7	8
Medicaid	1	2	2	2	3	3	3	4
Other	5	3	4	4	4	4	4	4
Net interest	3	3	3	3	4	5	6	16
Total	23	22	23	24	26	28	30	41
Deficit	2	3	3	4	6	8	10	20
Debt Held by the Public[a]	50	52	55	61	73	93	120	316
Memorandum:								
Gross Domestic Product (Trillions of dollars)	7.2	9.2	11.6	14.5	18.1	22.1	26.8	71.7

Notes: a. Consistent with the first official estimate for 1995 published March 4, 1996.
b. Discretionary spending is assumed to grow with net national product.
c. Fiscal Year.

Source: Congressional Budget Office (1996, May).

122

Table 8. Population of the United States, by Age, Selected Years, 1950-2070

	1950	1970	1990	2010	2030	2050
					Projections	
					2030	2050
In Millions						
Less than 20 Years Old	54	81	75	82	83	84
20 to 64 Years Old	93	113	153	166	192	202
65 Years and Older	13	21	32	40	68	75
Total	150	216	260	307	343	360
As a Percentage of Total Population						
Less than 20 Years Old	34	38	29	27	24	23
20 to 64 Years Old	58	53	59	60	56	56
65 Years and Older	8	10	12	13	20	21
Total	100	100	100	100	100	100
Memorandum:						
Ratio of People Age 20 to 64 to People Age 65 Years and Older	7.3	5.4	4.8	4.7	2.8	2.7

Note: Numbers may not add to totals because of rounding.

Source: Congressional Budget Office based on data from the Social Security Administration (1996, May).

123

Beginning in 2011, members of the baby boom generation will begin reaching age 65 at the rate of one every 8.5 seconds. By 2021, this rate will increase to one every 4.5 seconds. There are several ways to prevent this crisis in Social Security, which is already the largest single item in the federal budget. It should cost $348 billion this fiscal year.

One change that is most unlikely is to simply repeal Social Security. That would restore budget balance and even provide a surplus overnight, but it would also be likely to end the political careers of every member of Congress who voted for it along with that of the President. One potential change that has a good chance of being enacted is a reduction in the indexation formula. Under current law, Social Security payments are increased on January 1 every year by the percentage change in the consumer price index (CPI) the previous September in relation to its level one year earlier. This procedure is actuarially unsound and there are several proposals in Congress to change it to the CPI less some percentage, with these ranging from 0.5 to 3.0 percent. Enacting a change like this and spreading it to other indexed programs would go a long way toward avoiding the 2025 debacle scenario.

Another possibility is to significantly raise the age limit at which people could collect full Social Security benefits. Raising this gradually to the 70-75 years of age level would also pay great dividends in the future. Many analysts have suggested that Social Security should be partially privatized. This would make the program work like the one in Chile, which has had great success in raising both the personal savings rate and retirement incomes in that country. This plan would treat Social Security like a huge 401K (or 403B) program and would engender enormous increases in investment in the United States. Of course, the transition costs over 40 years or so would be extremely large and no one has a good idea of how to pay for these as yet.

Medicare is projected to cost $196 billion this fiscal year and it will balloon in the future for the same demographic reasons unless serious changes are made. The program is already running at a loss in 1996 and is currently projected to exhaust its trust fund by 2001.

Here, repeal is a more viable option. There is no economic theory that says that some citizens of the United States should pay 2.9 percent of their wages and salaries to provide heavily subsidized health care to other citizens simply because the recipient group is 65 years of age or older. It is more likely that a combination of rising copayments, tying benefits to income, and the use of health maintenance organizations will be tried first. However, the pressures to reduce Medicare spending will be with us for many years to come.

Table 6 shows the CBO estimates of the "fiscal dividend" that is forecast to arise from the enactment into law of credible balanced budget legislation. Most of the affects on the economy come from lower interest rates. If Congress were to enact The Economic Growth and Price Stability Act sponsored by Senator Connie Mack (R-Florida) and Representative Jim Saxton (R-New Jersey) that would give the Federal Open Market Committee (FOMC), the arm of the Federal Reserve System that sets monetary policy, the sole goal of achieving and maintaining price stability, then the outlook would be even more positive. Price stability is not defined as a measured inflation rate of zero in this legislation, but rather as a rate of inflation so low that it does not influence business or personal economic decisions.

Global evidence shows that countries that have low rates of inflation over long periods of time have the highest sustained rates of real economic growth. This legislation, if enacted, would be likely to lead to even lower interest rates since lenders would not have to demand such a premium to cover the risks of unanticipated inflation.

VIII. BALANCING THE BUDGET COULD IMPROVE ECONOMIC GROWTH

A credible budget balancing program that accomplished the goal through a combination of expenditure restraint and judicious tax reform that reduced the negative affects on savings and investment of the current tax system could actually result in increasing economic growth over the next 25 years and beyond. In the 1996 *Economic Report of the President*, the Council of Economic Advisers (CEA) demonstrates how deficit reduction lowers long term interest rates (Council of Economic Advisers, 1996, p. 70).

The most important channel of influence runs from the portfolio notion that a lower supply of government debt directly reduces real long term interest rates and spurs growth. There is also a fiscal drag channel to the degree that lower government spending is not offset by higher private sector expenditures. Finally, there is a term structure affect that acts to lower long term interest rates further as investors anticipate lower short-term interest rates in the future.

The CEA report goes on to discuss the critical role of investors in bond markets. If these "bond market vigilantes" think that the deficit reduction program is likely to succeed, they will bid up bond prices and thus lower long-term interest rates by more than short term rates fall. This affect occurred in the financial markets in 1995 and in 1996, when investors became worried that the balanced budget deal might fall apart, the 30-year Treasury yield briefly went back above 7.0 percent for the first time in over a year. It remains to be seen whether the "bond market vigilantes" will be able to force the Congress and President Clinton to agree on a viable budget balancing package.

IX. INTERNATIONAL COMPARISONS OF THE FISCAL PROBLEM

Well over half of the International Monetary Fund's (IMF) May, 1996, *World Economic Outlook* is devoted to discussions of fiscal policy with separate chapters for industrial countries, developing countries, and the countries in transition from communism or socialism to capitalism. A review of the material on industrial countries shows that many major

countries, such as Canada, France, Germany, Italy, and Japan
have far worse fiscal problems that those of the United States
(International Monetary Fund, 1996). Many readers may
remember the riots in France last December as a result of
proposals to reduce government pensions and slow the growth
of Social Security.

In all industrial countries, the problems arise from the fact
that expenditures have grown far faster than revenues and that
the share of the population represented by people 65 years of

Table 9.   Industrial Countries: Sustained 15-Year Changes in Primary
Government Balance Required to Stabilize Net Debt to GDP
(In percent of GDP)

	Net Debt		Primary Balance	Required Change in Primary Balance[a]	
	Average				
	1978-80	*1995*	*1995*	*Scenario 1*	*Scenario 2*
Austria	35.7	54.6	-2.6	4.8	5.2
Belgium	62.7	127.9	4.7	4.3	6.4
Canada	12.6	66.7	1.8	4.2	3.0
Denmark	2.3	54.5	1.7	3.4	1.5
France[b]	-0.6	35.1	-2.0	5.7	3.7
Germany[b]	11.0	49.1	-0.3	4.2	2.9
Ireland[b]	71.6	86.3	2.3	-1.7	1.1
Italy[b]	54.4	108.9	3.3	6.0	7.6
Japan[c]	14.4	9.8	-2.5	2.5	1.5
Netherlands	21.9	60.5	0.8	3.6	3.0
Norway	8.8	-21.5	-4.1	1.8	0.4
Spain[b]	5.2	50.3	-0.5	5.9	4.2
Sweden[b]	-19.5	27.0	-5.3	9.9	6.6
United Kingdom	46.3	40.8	-2.5	3.0	4.1
United States	25.6	56.4	0.5	2.3	2.0

Notes: [a] Scenario 1 shows the increase in the primary balance, starting in 1995, that would return
the ratio of net debt to GDP to the average of the 1978-1980 level by 2010. Scenario 2
shows the increase in the primary balance required for net debt to become 30 percent
of GDP by 2010.
[b] For these countries net debt data are taken from the OECD, Economic Outlook data base.
[c] Due to the large asset position of the Japanese social security fund, gross debt and the
net debt of the government are vastly different. The average gross debt over the period
1978-1980 was 46.9 percent of GDP, while in 1995 it was 87.0 percent of GDP. Using
these figures in the calculations would imply that the required change in the primary balance
to meet the objectives of scenario 1 and 2 would be 7.9 and 9.0 percent of GDP,
respectively.

Source: World Economic Outlook data base, International Monetary Fund (1996, May).

age or older is rising rapidly. The IMF staff estimates are that this global explosion in public debt over the past 15 years has increased real interest rates around the world by 1.0-2.5 percentage points or perhaps even more (International Monetary Fund, 1996, p. 70).

Budget analysts refer to the primary balance as the budget balance excluding interest payments on the national debt. Table 9 is a real shocker. For each country, it shows the sustained improvements in primary balances that would be required to return its net public debt from 1995 levels either to their average 1978-1980 levels or to move to an arbitrary level of 30 percent of GDP by the year 2010.

To follow Table 9 for the United States, which had a ratio of debt to GDP of 56.4 percent in 1995, we would have to run a primary budget surplus of 2.3 percent a year for the next 15 years to reduce the debt share to the 25.6 percent that prevailed from 1978-1980 or by 2.0 percent a year to get down to 30 percent. Other countries have even bigger tasks in front of them. It defies belief that Belgium, Italy or Sweden could pull off such massive shifts. It will take enormous political will power to get the United States to increase its primary balance to the 2.0-2.3 percent range.

The IMF suggests that there may be a virtuous circle between economic growth and debt-ratio reduction. This is particularly likely to be true if interest rates are lower, the economy keeps growing, and major trading partners are growing at a good pace (International Monetary Fund, 1996, p. 84).

For many macroeconomic policies, New Zealand has proven to be a most interesting role model. They have a monetary control act that requires the Governor of the Bank of New Zealand to pursue price stability as his only goal and his income is related to his degree of success in keeping inflation below 2.0 percent.

Similarly, they passed the Fiscal Responsibility Act in 1994. According to the IMF: "The principles of responsible fiscal policy defined by the Act include the achievement of 'prudent levels' of government debt through operational budget surpluses; the maintenance of prudent debt levels, once achieved, through balanced budgets on average over reasonable periods of time; the achievement and maintenance of adequate levels of government net worth to provide a buffer against future adverse developments; the prudent management of fiscal risks, including a buffer against future adverse development; the prudent management of fiscal risks, including pension liabilities; and the pursuit of expenditure policies consistent with stable and predictable tax rates. The Act avoids the problems of balanced budget rules that would preclude automatic stabilizers from operating. And the requirement that tax rates be stable and predictable reinforces the long-term orientation of fiscal policy and the need to budget for future liabilities.

The Act also requires the government to specify short-and long-term fiscal objectives that are consistent with the principles laid out. It allows the government to depart temporarily from these principles, provided they explain why and specify how and when they plan to return to them. The government has specified prudent levels of public sector debt to be below 30 percent of GDP in the short term and below 20 percent in the longer term.

The Act also improved the quality of information flows about the public finances. A major innovation was the requirement that all of the financial reporting and forecasts be prepared on a basis consistent with the private sector's generally accepted accounting practice. This was done to enhance the credibility of public sector accounts and also to take advantage of the synergies and economies that result from aligning public and private sector accounting practices."

"With the passage of its Fiscal Responsibility Act, New Zealand took a practical step to increase the fiscal transparency of its government decision and to promote responsible fiscal management. Similar approaches could be worth considering in other countries."

X. ANALYZING THE IMPACT ON BUSINESS FIRMS OF EFFORTS TO ACHIEVE A BALANCED BUDGET

Detailed analysis of the affects on any particular business firm depend at least partially on what its lines of business are. A company whose sole product is boots for military personnel would be critically affected by changes in procurement rates or rules and would be unlikely to worry a lot about macroeconomic affects such as changes in interest rates. There is no substitute for carefully analyzing what lines of business a firm is in and searching for government programs that directly affect the firm. Every year CBO publishes a tome that contains thousands of ways to reduce the deficit (Congressional Budget Office, 1996, August). Many of these budget changes have found their way into the pending legislation.

The true budgetary analyst can find several places on the World Wide Web to practice ways to reduce the budget or keep up to date on how fast the national debt is growing (Zuckerman, 1996). There is even a "Budget game" that one can play. It seems clear that the biggest impacts of a federal government budget that actually results in spending declines as a share of GDP are lower interest rates, higher savings and thus greater investment, faster rates of productivity growth, higher employment, higher disposable personal income, higher corporate profits, and probably a smaller trade deficit. While all of these things are good and would combine to improve the rate of growth of the U.S. economy, no one could possibly know in advance by how much.

Similarly, the impact on particular business firms will vary enormously. A full or partial privatization of Social Security would create many opportunities for money managers and for business firms to expand. A strong move to subject all regulatory activities to firm cost-benefit analysis could pay huge dividends to many firms. Most budget analysts forget that it is possible to accomplish most goals of "budget activists" almost as well by regulation as by increasing direct government expenditures.

In his marvelous book, *Rendezvous With Reality*, Murray Weidenbaum laid out a "dirty dozen" list of sensible ways to reduce government spending (Weidenbaum, 1988). He also pointed out that the best way to ensure that spending programs don't return is to completely eliminate them. We no longer have a Civil Aeronautics Board or an Interstate Commerce Commission. The latter was our oldest regulatory agency, having been founded in the Cleveland Administration in 1887. We even got rid of the tea tasting board in the 1996 Budget.

Most good budget analysts could tell you how to balance the budget in one year or less. Robert Barro had one very clear set of proposals to achieve balance quickly (Barro, 1993). Murray Weidenbaum's chapter in this book shows how cutting some government spending reaps a double dividend for the economy. Spending less on regulation not only helps the budget but also saves business firms the cost of compliance.

One should not await the arrival of a budget surplus at the federal level with baited breath. It could come in any year from 1999-2005. The real trick will be making the longer-term hard choices to ensure responsible fiscal management throughout at least the first half of the twenty-first century. Success in this endeavor can contribute a great deal to the continued prominence of the United States of America as an economy with no real peers on the global stage.

REFERENCES

Barro, R.J. (1993, May 26). Deficit reduction made easy. *The Wall Street Journal.*

Beard, C.A. (1935). *An economic interpretation of the constitution of the United States* (new Ed.). New York: The Macmillan Company.

Buchanan, J.M. (1989, January). On the structure of an economy: A reemphasis of some classical foundations. *Business Economics, XXIV*(1), 6-12.

Congressional Budget Office. (1996a). *The economic and budget outlook: Fiscal years 1997-2006.* Washington, DC: Government Printing Office.

Congressional Budget Office. (1996b). *The economic and budget outlook: April 1996 update* (A CBO Memorandum). Washington, DC: Government Printing Office.

Congressional Budget Office. (1995). *The economic and budget outlook: December 1995 update* (A CBO Memorandum). Washington, DC: Government Printing Office.

Congressional Budget Office. (1996, August). *Reducing the deficit: Spending and revenue options.* Washington, DC: Government Printing Office.

Council of Economic Advisers. (1995, December). *Economic indicators.* Washington, DC: Government Printing Office.

Council of Economic Advisers. (1996). *Economic report of the president.* Washington, DC: Government Printing Office.

International Monetary Fund. (1996). *World economic outlook: May, 1996.* Washington, DC: International Monetary Fund.

McCracken, P. (1995, December 26). Why deficits matter. *The Wall Street Journal.*

Moore, S. (1996). *Broken promises: What's gone wrong with the economy in the 1990s* (IPI Policy Report No. 136). Lewisville, TX: The Institute for Policy Innovation.

O'Neill, J.E. (1996). *Statement on the economic and budget outlook: Fiscal years 1997-2006 before the Committee on the Budget, U.S. House of Representatives.* Washington, DC: Congressional Budget Office.

Ott, D.J., & Ott, A.F. (1965). *Federal budget policy.* Washington, DC: The Brookings Institution.

Stein, H. (1989). *Governing the $5 trillion economy.* New York: Oxford University Press.

Stein, H. (1993, November 29). Needed: A budget policy. *The Wall Street Journal.*

Weidenbaum, M. (1988). *Rendezvous with reality.* New York: Basic Books.

Wildavsky, A, & Boskin, M.J. (Eds.). (1982). *Budgets as compromises among social orders' in the federal budget: Economics and politics.* San Francisco, CA: Institute for Contemporary Studies.

Zuckerman, L. (1996, January 1). Taking in the sites: A virtually balanced budget. *The New York Times.*

UNDERSTANDING A CONSUMPTION TAX AS FUNDAMENTAL TAX REFORM

R. Glenn Hubbard

I. INTRODUCTION

Fundamental tax reform—either reform of the income tax or a switch from the current tax system to a consumption tax system—is being hotly debated. The Committee on Ways and Means began hearings on fundamental tax reform in March 1996,[1] and will hold hearings throughout 1996 on economic issues, transition problems, and steps toward implementation of tax reform. Many analysts believe that 1997 or 1998 will witness very serious discussion in Congress of tax reform proposals.

Below I discuss some of the key problems in the current tax system prompting calls for fundamental tax reform. I then evaluate consumption taxes as an alternative to the current tax system.

Advances in the Study of Entrepreneurship, Innovation, and Economic Growth,
Volume 8, pages 133-146.
Copyright © 1996 by JAI Press Inc.
All rights of reproduction in any form reserved.
ISBN: 0-7623-0185-6

In that evaluation, I note that much of the gains in economic efficiency, simplicity, and fairness accomplished by moving from the current tax system to a broad-based consumption tax could also be accomplished by reform of the income tax. The *Appendix* to the paper describes similarities and differences among alternative consumption tax plans.

II. THE NEED FOR FUNDAMENTAL TAX REFORM

Current U.S. tax law distorts the allocation of the nation's capital stock and reduces saving and investment. To begin, current law treats corporations and their investors as separate entities. Under this so-called "classical" system of corporate taxation, two levels of tax are levied on earnings from investments in corporate equity. First, income earned by corporations is taxed at the corporate level. Second, when the corporation distributes dividends to shareholders, the income is taxed at the shareholder level as ordinary income. Undistributed earnings, which increase share values, are also double taxed, since they are taxed at capital gains rates when shares are sold.

In contrast, investors who conduct business activity in noncorporate form, such as a sole proprietorship or partnership (or in corporate form through an *S* corporation), are taxed once on their earnings at their individual tax rate. Corporate earnings distributed as interest to suppliers of debt capital are generally taxed to U.S. taxpayers as ordinary income. However, interest paid is generally deductible by the corporation, and thus not subject to tax at the corporate level.

"Integration" of the corporate and individual income taxes refers to any plan in which corporate income is taxed only once, rather than taxed both when earned and when distributed to shareholders as dividends. Integration has many variants. In January 1992, the U.S. Treasury Department released a study of corporate tax integration, *Integration of the Individual and Corporate Tax Systems*. The American Law Institute also released a report on integration. The two reports document the economic distortions caused by the current two-tier tax system and the need to change the way in which the United States taxes corporations and their shareholders, and presents the issues involved with alternative approaches.

Despite their differences, methods of integration reflect a common goal: To the extent practicable, fundamental economic considerations, not the tax structure, should guide investment, organizational, and financial decisions. Although the Tax Reform Act of 1986 reduced the effect of taxation on many business decisions, that reform did not directly address distortions in business organizational and financing decisions under current law. Thus, integration can be viewed as the next logical step in tax reform.

The current system of business income taxation raises questions of fairness because it creates differences in the taxation of alternative sources of income from capital. A taxpayer conducting an equity-financed business in corporate form faces a different tax burden than a taxpayer conducting the same business in noncorporate form. A corporation that raises capital in the form of equity faces a different tax burden than a corporation that raises the same amount of capital from debt. A similar disparity exists in the treatment of corporations that finance investment with retained earnings and those that pay dividends and finance investment with new equity. Because of its bias towards debt, the current tax system encourages taxpayers to engage in practices that tend to disguise equity as debt. This effort represents a wasteful use of resources, and imposes significant administrative costs in attempting to distinguish debt from equity. These arguments for integrating the corporate and individual income tax systems have been put forth by economists and legal specialists for more than a generation. Three factors have maintained tax integration's place in the tax reform debate over the past decade.

First, the 1980s witnessed an explosion of corporate borrowing in the United States. Indeed, many observers believe that this activity—and the accompanying financial distress it brought in many sectors of the economy—was influenced significantly by the tax bias against equity finance. While the greatest reliance on debt had its origin in many factors, the use of debt contracts with virtually no provisions to index repayments to shifts in industry-wide or economy-wide conditions almost surely reflects the tax preference given such debt under current law. Financial decisions, which may leave firms more vulnerable to a downturn in the economy, should be based on fundamental economic considerations, not the tax code. The tax bias against equity finance needs to be addressed.

Second, these distortions have economic costs. Integration of the individual and corporate tax systems would reduce or eliminate these economic distortions. The potential economic gains could be substantial, as suggested in the Treasury Report.

Third, aside from these efficiency gains, the various integration prototypes, especially those that also focus on the taxation of interest, provide a mechanism for addressing a problem which has increasingly troubled many governments—the difficulty of taxing income from capital in a global economy. It is desirable to keep the overall tax rate on income from capital as low as possible. However, the ability of some investors to avoid or reduce taxation of capital income, while other investors cannot, is not an adequate surrogate for a uniform lower rate of taxation on all income from capital.

Finally, the thrust of integration on tax reform—taxing income once—still leaves a single level of tax on capital income. Many economists believe that the resulting intertemporal distortions of household saving decisions and business investment decisions are large, reducing growth opportunities and economic efficiency.

III. A CONSUMPTION TAX AS FUNDAMENTAL TAX REFORM

The term "consumption tax" actually applies to a range of tax systems. The base of a broad-based consumption tax is households' consumption, not households' net income. "Consumption taxes" can be collected from businesses, households, or both. They can be familiar sales taxes, but do not have to be. Further, consumption taxes can incorporate exemptions and graduated marginal tax rates, as under the income tax. Many economists support the use of consumption taxes to replace the current individual and corporate income taxes. This support reflects efficiency, fairness, and simplicity concerns.

The nation would enjoy three sources of efficiency gains from moving to a broad-based consumption tax. First, the removal of the current tax on returns to new saving and investment increases capital accumulation and, ultimately, household incomes.[2] Second, the consumption tax removes distortions in the allocation of capital across sectors and types of capital. Third, a broad-based consumption tax avoids potentially costly distortions of firms' financial and organizational structure.[3] Taken together, efficiency gains from moving to a consumption tax are potentially dramatic. Professor Dale Jorgenson of Harvard University estimates the present value of growth opportunities created by the move from the 1985 to law to the Tax Reform Act of 1986 to be about $1 trillion (1987 dollars). Jorgenson also estimates that, had the United States moved from the 1985 income tax law to a broad-based consumption tax, gains in growth opportunities would have doubled to about $2 trillion. The additional gains are due to leveling the playing field and to expensing business investment.

With respect to fairness, many economists believe that consumption represents a better measure of "ability to pay" than does current income, because households' consumption decisions depend on wealth and expected future income as well as current income. Finally, a properly designed broad-based consumption tax promotes simplicity. Several consumption tax systems avoid much of the costly complexity associated with the present income tax.

IV.   STEPS TOWARD FUNDAMENTAL TAX REFORM

How might we move from the current tax system to a broad-based consumption tax? What aspects of reform generate significant improvements in efficiency, simplicity, and fairness? To fix ideas, I focus on the "flat tax" proposal of Robert Hall and Alvin Rabushka of the Hoover Institution.[4] While I abstract from many details of the proposal and from transition complications, I show in Table 1 that it is possible to characterize this fundamental tax

Table 1.   Moving from the Current Tax System to a Consumption Tax

Steps 1-3:   Integrate the tax system.

Step 1:   End the double taxation of corporate equity returns.
Integrate the corporate and individual tax systems by excluding dividends from taxable income at the individual level (Treasury proposal) or by fully crediting taxes paid at the corporate level to recipients of dividends (American Law Institute proposal). Eliminate the capital gains tax on accumulated retained earnings.

Step 2:   End the tax bias against equity finance in favor of debt finance.
Collect the tax on returns to debt at the entity level by disallowing business deductions for interest payments and removing interest receipts from taxable income at the individual level (Treasury proposal).

Step 3:   Consolidate reporting of business income for tax purposes.
Report all business income on a single business tax form—including income currently reported from sole proprietorships, partnerships, rental property, and Subchapter S corporations (Treasury proposal). Note: Because we eliminated the corporate/noncorporate business distinction in Step 1, all businesses can use the same tax form.

Steps 4-7:   Broaden the base and lower the rates.

Step 4:   Broaden the base of the business tax.
Eliminate any preferential tax provisions for particular industries and firms. Repeal the alternative minimum tax.

Step 5:   Collect taxes on employee fringe benefits at the business level.
Disallow business deductions for expenditures on employee fringe benefits. Remove tax liability for such benefits from the individual tax.

Step 6:   Broaden the base of the individual tax.
Eliminate all itemized deductions, the standard deduction, and any adjustments to gross income. Repeal the alternative minimum tax.

Step 7:   Lower marginal tax rates on individuals and businesses.
Replace the graduated-rate individual tax system with a system with a single rate. Reduce the business tax rate to the same single rate as the individual tax rate. To maintain progressivity, retain and expand the generosity of the personal exemption. Note: A refundable individual tax credit could also be added for low-income households.

Steps 8-9:   Move to a consumption tax.

Step 8:   Replace accrual accounting for businesses with cash flow accounting.
Allow expensing for all purchases from other firms including purchases of capital assets.

Step 9:   Shift from a residence-based tax system to a territorial tax system.
Remove foreign-source income from the U.S. tax base.

reform as a nine-step process. While each step represents a significant change in tax policy, virtually all of the steps are consistent with fundamental *income* tax reform. Moreover, many of the steps to reform have been advanced for many years by economists and policymakers. I consider the steps in turn below under three themes: (1) integrating the corporate and individual tax, (2) broadening the base and reducing marginal tax rates, and (3) moving to consumption taxation.

A.   Integrating the Corporate and Individual Income Tax

The first three steps toward fundamental tax reform integrate the corporate and individual tax system. Step 1 ends the double taxation of corporate equity returns. The Treasury Department's integration report recommended a dividend exclusion prototype for dividend relief. Under this prototype, corporations would pay the corporate income tax, computing taxable income in the same way as under current law. However, dividends paid would not be taxed again at the investor level. The Treasury model also ended double taxation of retained earnings by allowing shareholders to increase stock basis for retained earnings, thereby avoiding a subsequent capital gains tax on retained earnings.

Step 2 ends the tax bias against equity finance in favor of debt finance. The Treasury Department's integration study proposed to accomplish this by extending the dividend exclusion prototype to interest. Treasury's model—the Comprehensive Business Income Tax (CBIT)—would apply to all businesses, noncorporate and corporate. Under CBIT, neither deductions for payments to debtholders nor to shareholders would be permitted, and a tax would be collected at the entity level (at a rate equal to the highest marginal individual tax rate). However, both interest and equity distributions would be excludable from income by investors. Step 3, which would consolidate reporting of business income for tax purposes, would be accomplished by a proposal such as CBIT.

B.   Broadening the Tax Base and Reducing Marginal Tax Rates

The next four steps implement the maxim guiding the Tax Reform Act of 1986—"broaden the base and lower the rates." Step 4 broadens the base of the business tax by eliminating preferential tax provisions for particular industries and firms and by repealing the alternative minimum tax. Step 5 continues the theme of "taxing income once" by collecting taxes on employee fringe benefits at the business level. In practice, this could be accomplished by disallowing business deductions for expenditures on employee fringe benefits and removing tax liability for such benefits from the individual tax. Step 6 broadens the base of the individual tax—eliminating all itemized deductions, the standard deduction, and any adjustments to gross income and repealing the alternative minimum tax. Having accomplished base broadening under the income tax, one can lower marginal rates on individuals and businesses. In practice, this could be accomplished by replacing the graduated-rate individual tax system with a single-rate system and reducing the business tax rate to the same single rate as the individual tax rate. To maintain progressivity, one could retain and expand the generosity of the personal exemption. A refundable individual tax credit could also be added for low-income households.

Steps 1-7 attempt to accomplish broad-based *income* tax reform by taxing income exactly once, broadening the tax base, and reducing marginal rates. These steps have, in one form or another been advocated by many economists and policymakers for many years. Enacting tax reform that embraced the missions of these steps would stimulate saving and investment, significantly reduce tax distortions of financing and organization decisions, and improve the efficiency with which the nation's capital stock is allocated.

C.   Moving to Consumption Taxation

It is only in Step 8 that we begin to introduce fundamental *consumption* tax reform. After the first seven steps, the tax base is (approximately) employee compensation plus business income (receipts less the sum of expenditures, compensation, materials, and depreciation of capital assets). The tax base under the consumption tax should be employee compensation plus business cash flow. Accordingly, Step 8 replaced accrual accounting for businesses with cash flow accounting. Most important, this step allows expensing for all purchases from other firms including purchases of capital assets. Relative to the business income tax, the move to expensing exempts from taxation the return on marginal investment projects—projects for which expected returns just cover the opportunity cost of funds.[5] Economic profits—based on entrepreneurial skill or good fortune—are taxed equally in the business income tax and in the business cash flow tax.[6]

The first eight steps essentially treat the United States as a closed economy. A broad-based consumption tax would not tax overseas income of U.S. enterprises. Hence Step 9 shifts the tax base from a residence-based tax system to a territorial tax system. This step would remove foreign-source income from the U.S. tax base.[7]

As I noted earlier, enacting the set of nine steps would lead to large gains in economic efficiency, simplicity, and tax fairness. It is important to note that even if one wanted to enact all nine—and move to a broad-based consumption tax such as the flat tax—significant gains can be accomplished by focusing on themes of "taxing income once" and "broadening the base and lowering the rates."

APPENDIX: DESIGNING A BROAD-BASED CONSUMPTION TAX

The discussion below reviews salient features of four consumption tax system: (1) a retail sales tax, (2) a value-added tax, (3) a two-tiered cash flow tax, and (4) a full-fledged personal cash flow tax. The first two systems collect revenue only from businesses, while the last two collect revenue from households and businesses. As broad-based consumption taxes, each is borne by consumption. While, under some conditions, these systems are roughly equivalent in their economic effects, they differ in their ease of administration and in their ability to achieve objectives for progressivity.

I. OPTIONS FOR A BROAD-BASED CONSUMPTION TAX

A. Taxes Collected from Businesses

Retail Sales Tax

Perhaps the most familiar "consumption tax" in the public imagination is the retail sales tax, in which tax is collected on businesses' sales of goods and services to households. Most states have retail sales taxes. As a broad-based consumption tax, a retail sales tax should exempt sales between businesses and tax all goods and services. Conventional state-level sales taxes are not broad-based consumption taxes because they generally do not apply to all forms of consumption (for example, food and health care expenditures and certain services). Only domestic consumers pay the retail sales tax, so that it taxes imports and exempts exports.

Two-Tiered Cash Flow Tax

The two-tiered cash flow tax involves two tax-collecting vehicles, a business tax and an individual compensation tax. The coordinated use of these two instruments allows one to tax consumption at different rates for different people.

Calculating the business tax base begins with value added (sales less purchases from other firms), as with value-added taxes. In a cash flow tax, payments to workers (for current, past, or future labor services) are deducted. Investment is expensed, so there are no depreciation allowances. Similarly, no interest is deductible. Firms then pay a flat rate of tax on the final amount, cash flow.

The base for the individual tax is the set of payments received by individuals for current, past, and future labor services. Capital income is not taxed. The rate of individual tax could be flat or graduated, and further progressivity can be incorporated by adding an exemption.

One popular variant, the Simple Flat Tax of Robert Hall and Alvin Rabushka, in which the business and individual tax share a common flat marginal rate, is related to a value-added tax. Under a value-added tax, payments for compensation are not deductible by businesses, but they are not taxed for individuals. Under the Simple Flat Tax, payments for compensation are deductible by businesses, but taxable for individuals. If the businesses and individual marginal rates are identical, the value-added tax and the simple flat tax are identical, if the flat tax has no individual exemption. This is not a coincidence, of course. It is a consequence of the fact that they are different ways of taxing the same base—personal consumption. Progressivity can be introduced by allowing an exemption. Other variants of the two-tiered cash flow tax can incorporate graduated marginal rates.

While "pure" two-tiered cash flow taxes do not embody deductions, it is possible to include certain deductions in a consistent manner. Because the objective is to design a consumption tax, allowing interest deductions would be inconsistent. However, deductions for state and local taxes or charitable contributions, if desired, are consistent with the approach. The costs of such deductions are additional complexity and the need for a higher rate of tax on the remaining tax base.

Full-Fledged Personal Cash-Flow Tax

A full-fledged cash flow tax (or "consumed income tax") would be collected solely from individuals. The tax base is a cash flow rather than the current accrued-income base. Individuals pay tax on reported cash flow less net saving. Because consumption equals the difference between income and net saving, the base of the personal cash flow tax is consumption. While saving is deductible, proceeds from borrowing, as a cash inflow, are included in the base to measure cash flow properly. A personal cash flow tax can incorporate a flat rate, an exemption and flat marginal rate, or an exemption and graduated marginal rates.

A full-fledged personal cash-flow tax allows elimination of the corporate income tax. With cash flow tax treatment, individual shareholders are permitted a deduction for the purchase of shares; dividends and the value of shares sold are included in taxable cash flow. Similar treatment is given to partnership and proprietorship organizations. Partners and proprietors pay tax on net cash flow; cash receipts are included in the base, and net contributions are deducted.

Under some circumstances, the personal consumption tax and the two-tiered cash flow tax discussed earlier are equivalent. If there were no exemptions and businesses and individual taxpayers pay tax at a uniform rate, the systems are equivalent. This equivalence assumes that all financial transactions are in the tax base.

One drawback of full-fledged personal cash flow taxes is administrative burden. For example, the government would have to monitor returns on savings deducted by taxpayers in the past. It is possible to limit this monitoring problem by requiring funds to be placed in qualified accounts (for example, accounts maintained by financial intermediaries or pension plans or closely held businesses). Dealing with fringe benefits is also more difficult in a personal consumption tax than in a two-tiered cash flow tax. On the one hand, under a personal consumption tax, a value of employee fringe benefits would have to be included in the employee's taxable cash flow. On the other hand, under a two-tiered cash flow tax, denial of a deduction at the entity level can replace the inclusion of fringe benefits in the individual tax base.

II.   IMPLICATIONS FOR DESIGN OF A BROAD-BASED CONSUMPTION TAX

A. Goals

- Achieving the *efficiency* goal of moving to a consumption tax requires the selection of the broadest possible tax base: *A desirable system should not make it easy to have different rates of tax for different goods and services.*
- Achieving the *fairness* goal of moving to a consumption tax requires the ability to make the system progressive. Retail sales taxes and VATs alone are unlikely to be fair in this sense.
- Achieving the *simplicity* goal of moving to a consumption tax requires reduction in complexity (and rent-seeking activities) associated with the current income tax: *A desirable system should not extend information and monitoring requirements beyond those associated with the current in come tax (and, hopefully, would reduce them).*

B.   Steps Toward Designing a Proposal

A two-tiered cash flow tax—such as the simple flat tax or a business transfer tax plus a wage tax—probably comes closest to achieving efficiency, fairness, and simplicity goals of the reform. Such a tax is also more likely to be politically acceptable than a uniform sales tax or value-added tax because progressivity can be maintained even under current rules for distributional analysis.

NOTES

1.   This paper was presented as testimony to the Committee in its general hearing on March 27, 1996.

2.   Many economists have argued that switching from an income tax to a consumption tax significantly increases saving and capital accumulation. This is because a consumption tax exempts returns to new saving, thereby increasing households' willingness to save. In the early 1980s, Lawrence Summers, currently Deputy Secretary of the Treasury Department, concluded that a move to a consumption tax would lead to major increases in capital accumulation and economic well being (see Summers, 1981).

There are two reasons to suspect that gains in saving may be smaller than researchers originally guessed. The first is that the current "income" tax already embodies some elements of a consumption tax. For example, saving through pension plans, IRAs, Keoghs, or 401(k) arrangements already enjoy cash flow treatment. In addition, investment incentives offer a form of partial expensing. Second, recent research on saving suggests that a significant function of household saving is "precautionary saving" against uncertainty over future earnings, medical expenses, or length of life as opposed to saving for retirement *per se*. Such saving decisions are less influenced by changes in the after-tax interest rates than retirement saving decisions, implying a smaller overall response of saving to tax reform. Nonetheless, combining these two caveats, a recent Brookings Institution study concluded that saving rates would fall by between 5 and 10 percent (see Engen & Gale, 1996).

Another reason that many economists and policymakers favor fundamental tax reform emphasizing consumption taxation over income taxation is that such reform may stimulate business investment. Under the current income, tax businesses are permitted to depreciate capital investment over time. Under a consumption tax, investment is expensed. Under current law, the present value of one dollar of depreciation allowance is about $0.83 for equipment investment; under expensing, that present value is, of course, $1.00. In a study of effects of the cost of capital on investment, Kevin Hassett and I estimate that this change would raise the annual business equipment rate by 10 percent (see Hassett & Hubbard, 1996).

3.   Distortions in the allocation of capital and in financial and organizational structure can also be reduced through fundamental income tax reform. The

Treasury Department's 1992 study of corporate tax integration study estimated increases in economic well-being from integration in many cases as large as gains accompanying reforms in the Tax Reform Act of 1986. The gains result from improved allocation of real resources, reductions in the likelihood of firms experiencing financial distress, and the shift toward allowing corporations to make capital structure and dividend decisions based on nontax benefits and costs (see U.S. Department of the Treasury, 1992).

4.   In the *Appendix* of this testimony, I offer a brief comparison of alternative forms of broad-based consumption taxes and arguments for favoring the flat tax over a value-added tax or a national retail sales tax.

5.   One could also implement a broad-based consumption tax by taxing compensation once at the business level by using a subtraction-method value-added tax. Relative to Step 8, this would require eliminating the individual tax and disallowing businesses' deductions of payments to labor.

6.   For a general discussion of this point, see Gentry and Hubbard (1996).

7.   One can also make a principled argument for moving to a territorial tax system as part of fundamental income tax reform (see Hubbard, 1995).

REFERENCES

Engen, E., & Gale, W. (1996, February). *The effects of fundamental tax reform on saving* (Mimeo.). Washington, DC: The Brookings Institutions.

Gentry, W.M., & Hubbard, R.G. (1996, March). *Distributional implications of moving to a broad-based consumption tax* (Mimeo.). Columbia University.

Hassett, K.A. & Hubbard, R.G. (1996, January). *Tax policy and investment* (Mimeo.). Columbia University.

Hubbard, R.G. (1995). U.S. tax policy and foreign direct investment: Incentives, problems, and reform. In *Tax policy and economic growth*. Washington, DC: American Council for Capital Formation.

Summers, L.H. (1981, September). Capital taxation and accumulation in a life-cycle growth model. *American Economic Review, 71*, 533-544.

U.S. Department of the Treasury. (1992). *Integration of the individual and corporate tax systems: Taxing business income once*. Washington, DC: U.S. Government Printing Office.

FORECASTING U.S. ECONOMIC TRENDS FOR USE BY MID-SIZE BUSINESS:
THE ROLE OF THE FEDERAL RESERVE

Donald A. Wells

I. INTRODUCTION

Mid-size companies typically don't have direct access to economics staff or to economic consultants. It would be useful for them to have some basis for making judgments about the future direction of national economic activity and financial markets. The purpose of this chapter is to provide guidelines to help owners and managers of mid-size businesses make these judgments. The ability to anticipate trends in the economy can contribute to better

Advances in the Study of Entrepreneurship, Innovation, and Economic Growth,
Volume 8, pages 147-168.
Copyright © 1996 by JAI Press Inc.
All rights of reproduction in any form reserved.
ISBN: 0-7623-0185-6

management and improved firm viability. The emphasis will be to analyze trends in the economy rather than focusing on day-to-day or week-to-week developments. A time horizon of 6 months to a year will help companies anticipate the overall prospects for GDP, interest rates, and consumer incomes, as examples. This time horizon contrasts with much of the reporting of economic news. The focus in the financial press is on the daily behavior of stock and bond prices, interest rates, and the "daily economic item worthy of a headline." For non-financial businesses, the plethora of data on a daily basis is likely to be more confusing than helpful.

Observing Federal Reserve policies and actions is a feasible approach for predicting the future behavior of the U.S. economy. There is no intent here to develop a precise forecast; sophisticated econometric models do not accomplish that, either. Shocks to the economic system—a major disruption of oil markets, a meltdown in the stock market, the bubonic plague—can make any forecasting hazardous. The advantage of such shocks from the viewpoint of the forecaster is that they offer ready and understandable explanations as to why a forecast was wrong. In this paper, we're looking for a few indicators that offer reasonable insight about the future course of economic activity.

II.   THE GENERAL APPROACH

The approach of this chapter is predicated on three propositions:

1.   Federal Reserve policies as they affect the monetary base and the money supply provide a reliable guide to future aggregate expenditures and the effects on national output and prices.
2.   Trends in interest rates can be established by using the analysis developed in (1), above. Because most mid-size companies are dependent on credit markets for working capital and capital expansion, interest rate trends are especially important to these companies, many of which are private and which do not have access to all the financial markets accessed by large public companies.

3. Information on Federal Reserve policies is readily available to lay persons in a timely manner and in a form that makes it relatively easy to utilize this information in the analysis discussed in this paper.

This overall assessment of the behavior of the national economy merely provides a backdrop for decisions by individual businesses. Individual industries, product lines, and regions must be factored into analyses of trends in national economic activity. For a rapidly growing company, a decline in Gross Domestic Product (GDP) may only slow down the growth of company sales. Each business must judge the tie-ins between the national economy and its own prospects. But few firms are likely to be able to divorce their own performance from overall economic activity. A feel for future trends in the U.S. economy should be part of decision making by individual businesses.[1]

For an approach to be helpful, it must rely on information that is readily accessible and easily understood. Owners and managers of mid-size businesses typically cannot devote much time to collecting and analyzing economic data. Similarly, the analysis must be basic and straight forward (simplified but not simple minded). Such an approach is useful only for basic trends in the behavior of overall production, prices, and interest rates. The test will be whether of not it is helpful to owners and managers of mid-size businesses.

Federal Reserve policies play a decisive role in establishing basic trends in the U.S. economy. These trends reflect the availability of money and credit, and the Federal Reserve plays the decisive role in determining this availability. The globalization of economic activity and financial markets has made the conduct of monetary policy more complicated and it conditions the impacts of Federal Reserve actions, but ultimately the Federal Reserve has a unique and powerful role in influencing the behavior of U.S. GDP and prices.

III. A PRIMER OF FEDERAL RESERVE POLICY

The typical introduction to Federal Reserve policy offers three major policy tools:

1. Reserve requirement changes;
2. Changes in the discount rate; and
3. Open market operations.

Reserve requirements stipulate the percentage of checkable deposit liabilities that banks must hold as reserves (which are vault cash and balances kept with the Federal Reserve). For most banks the reserve requirement on checkable accounts is 10 percent (Board of Governors of the Federal Reserve System, 1996, p. A97). This 10 percent reserve requirement has not changed since April 1992, a clear indication that reserve requirement changes are not an active policy tool of the Federal Reserve.

Discount rate changes receive considerable media attention and the announcement effect does have an immediate impact on short-term interest rates and financial markets in general. The discount rate is the interest rate charged by the Federal Reserve when banks borrow reserves. At 5 percent in March 1996, the discount rate was raised four times in the period from May 1994 to February 1995, but over almost a two year period from July 1992 to May 1994 the discount rate had remained at 3.5 percent (Board of Governors of the Federal Reserve System, 1996, p. A8).

Because the discount rate is changed only periodically and because bank borrowing of reserves from the Federal Reserve is small, the discount rate has little effect on the amount of bank reserves and subsequently on the money supply. When banks borrow reserves, rather than borrowing from the Federal Reserve they prefer to borrow in the federal funds market.[2] This market refers to overnight loans between banks of their reserve deposits at the Federal Reserve. Banks with excess reserves lend them to banks experiencing temporary shortfalls of reserves. It is a large market, with daily lending typically exceeding $60 billion. By contrast, bank borrowings from the Federal Reserve usually total less than $1 billion. The Federal Funds rate, the interest rate charged on these overnight loans, is a market determined rate reflecting the availability of bank reserves. If the trend of the federal funds rate is upward it signifies that bank reserves are tight relative to bank demand for reserves, and *vice versa*. Often Federal Reserve changes in the discount rate lag and follow changes in the federal funds rate, and a Federal Reserve announcement of a discount rate change often only confirms and validates a trend in the federal funds rate. Because the federal funds rate reflects the availability of bank reserves, and the Federal Reserve determines this availability through open market operations, the key to understanding the direction of Federal Reserve policy is to follow the results of its open market operations.

Open market operations refers to Federal Reserve purchases and sales of U.S. Treasury securities. Purchases increase bank reserves; sales reduce them. In turn, changes in bank reserves affect bank lending. An increase in reserves spurs lending and expands the supply of money. Decreases in reserves have the opposite effect. The most immediate impact of open market operations is to change the monetary base. The monetary base is defined as the reserves of the banking system plus U.S. currency. It is the best measure, albeit a rough one, of the direction of Federal Reserve policy as it impacts on the availability of money. Currency in the hands of the public, plus checkable deposits, constitute the narrowest measure of money (*M1*).

The Federal Reserve does not control the rate of withdrawals of currency from the banking system. Currency withdrawals reduce the deposits component of the money supply made possible by bank lending. The public determines the level of currency withdrawals by its preference for holding its money in the form of currency rather than as bank deposits. However, the Federal Reserve can offset currency withdrawals by increasing its open market purchases and adding more reserves to the banking system.

If the currency withdrawn from the banking system remains in the United States, it continues to finance spending in this country, but as much as 60 percent of the increase in United States currency ends up outside the United States. There is strong foreign demand for U.S. financial assets, and currency is one component of that demand. Because foreign ownership of currency does not contribute directly to expenditures in this country, the change in the monetary base might be weakened as an indicator of future expenditures in the United States. If the proportion of currency that goes abroad remains relatively constant, however, rates of change in the monetary base are good measures of the potential for rates of change of total expenditures in the United States.

An increase in the monetary base provides for an increase in the money supply. But the definition of the money supply is more ambiguous that 15 years ago. Money is a set of assets generally accepted when we make purchases. There are two major categories of these assets; one is *M1*, the more narrow measure of the amount of money, and the second is *M2*, a broader measure.

M1 consists primarily of currency in circulation and checkable deposits. *M2* includes *M1* plus small time deposits, savings deposits, money market deposit accounts, and money market mutual funds. In February 1996, *M1* measured $1,117 billion and *M2* was $3,690 billion. The measure of money most significant for the analysis of this paper is the one that is the best predictor of total spending on goods and services. 15 years ago, *M1* had a reasonably close relationship to GDP, but with the changes in banking laws in the early 1980s and the growing proliferation of financial assets, particularly those that are near money, *M2* has become a better measurement than *M1* for predicting spending and GDP. Assets included in *M2* but not in *M1* are easily converted into currency and checkable deposits,

Table 1.   Measures of the Money Supply

	February (billions of $)
M1 $1,117	
Currency	$373
Checkable Deposits	$745
M2 $3,690	
M1	$1,117
Savings Deposits	1.166
Small Time Deposits	934
Money Market Accounts	475

Source: Barron's (1996, April 1).

and the higher interest rates on these assets have induced the public to hold a higher proportion of their liquid assets in these near monies. *M2* also has the advantage that the movement of currency in and out of the United States has less influence on the measurement of *M2* relative to *M1*. From February 1995 to February 1996, *M2* increased from $3,517 billion to $3,690 billion, an increase of 4.9 percent.

Do changes in the monetary base (*MB*) approximate those of *M2*? The answer is, not exactly. Table 2 shows the relative changes of the monetary base and *M2* over three periods during 1994-1995.

Over the full eighteen-month period there is a rough approximation, an increase of 3.8 percent for the monetary base and 3.3 percent for *M2*. But for the two twelve-month periods shown in Table 2, from 6/1994 to 6/1995 *M2* increased by less than half of the increase in the monetary base, while from 12/1994 to 12/1995 *M2* increased considerably more than the monetary base. Thus the monetary base is a reasonable predictor of the direction of changes of *M2* but only a rough indicator of the magnitude of changes. Owners and managers of mid-size companies should look at both variables for trends in the availability of money. Information on the monetary base and the money supply are readily accessible in both *The Wall Street Journal* and *Barron's*. But an excellent source is *Monetary Trends*, published by the Federal Reserve Bank of St. Louis.[3] Tables 3 and 4 show the "triangles" that present compound annual rates of change for the monetary base and *M2*. Simply matching the initial month to the terminal month presents the rate of change for that period.

Table 2.   Changes in the Monetary Base and the Money Supply

Period	Percentage Change for MB	Percentage Change for M2
6/94-6/95	+ 5.3	+ 2.3
12/94-12/95	+ 3.2	+ 4.6
6/94-12/95	+ 3.8	+ 3.3

Source: The Federal Reserve Bank of St. Louis (1996, pp. 5, 7).

IV. AGGREGATE SPENDING AND GDP

Aggregate expenditures on final goods and services both measure GDP and are used to analyze its behavior. There are two basic approaches for analyzing aggregate expenditures. One, the Keynesian approach, studies the sum of consumption spending, investment spending, government purchases of goods and services, and net exports (exports minus imports). The second, the monetarist approach, studies the availability of money and the rate at which money is spent on goods and services (the velocity of money). Both approaches contribute to an understanding of the behavior of aggregate expenditures, GDP, and prices. This paper emphasizes the monetarist approach because it offers the nonprofessional a relatively simple way to predict trends in U.S. economic activity. The equation of exchange, developed by Irving Fisher more than 80 years ago (Fisher, 1963) and reinvigorated by Milton Friedman beginning in the 1950s (Friedman & Schwartz, 1963) provides a framework for looking at aggregate expenditures and aggregate output.

The rate of change of aggregate expenditures is made up of two components, the rate of change of the availability of money plus the rate of change of velocity. The rate of change of output is composed of the rate of change of real GDP plus the rate of change of prices (P). Expressed simply, percent change of $M2$ + percent change of V = percent change of GDP + percent change of P. The left-hand side of the equation is aggregate expenditures and the right hand side is aggregate output, both expressed in nominal (money value) terms.

Change in the amount of money is the primary determinant of change in spending. Except during the extremes of severe recession or depression or of substantial inflation, velocity will not be the major factor in explaining increases or decreases in total spending. Sophisticated economic analysis will examine the behavior of velocity carefully, but for the purposes of this paper velocity will be regarded as relatively stable.[8] Changes in the monetary base and thus the money supply will be the measures used to forecast changes in total spending.

Table 3. Adjusted Monetary Base
(Compound Annual Rates of Change)

Initial Month

Terminal Month	6-94	7-94	8-94	9-94	10-94	11-94	12-94	1-95	2-95	3-95	4-95	5-95	6-95	7-95	8-95	9-95	10-95	11-95	12-95	Billions of Dollars
7-94	7.3																			445.7
8-94	6.8	6.4																		448.0
9-94	6.5	6.1	5.8																	450.1
10-94	6.4	6.1	6.0	6.3																452.4
11-94	6.2	6.0	5.8	5.9	5.4															454.4
12-94	5.7	5.4	5.2	5.0	4.3	3.2														455.6
1-95	6.0	5.8	5.7	5.7	5.5	5.5	7.9													458.5
2-95	6.0	5.8	5.8	5.7	5.6	5.7	6.9	5.9												460.7
3-95	6.5	6.4	6.4	6.5	6.6	6.9	8.1	8.3	10.6											464.6
4-95	6.4	6.3	6.3	6.4	6.4	6.6	7.4	7.3	7.9	5.3										466.6
5-95	6.2	6.1	6.0	6.1	6.0	6.1	6.7	6.4	6.6	4.6	3.9									468.1
6-95	5.3	5.2	5.1	5.0	4.8	4.7	5.0	4.4	4.0	1.9	0.3	-3.3								466.8
7-95	4.9	4.8	4.6	4.5	4.3	4.2	4.3	3.7	3.3	1.5	0.3	-1.5	0.3							466.9
8-95	4.8	4.7	4.5	4.4	4.2	4.1	4.2	3.7	3.3	1.9	1.0	0.1	1.8	3.4						468.2
9-95	4.6	4.4	4.3	4.2	4.0	3.8	3.9	3.4	3.0	1.8	1.1	0.4	1.7	2.5	1.5					468.8
10-95	4.4	4.2	4.2	3.9	3.7	3.6	3.6	3.1	2.8	1.7	1.1	0.6	1.6	2.0	1.3	1.0				469.2
11-95	4.0	3.8	3.6	3.5	3.3	3.1	3.1	2.6	2.2	1.2	0.7	0.1	0.8	1.0	0.2	-0.5	-2.0			468.4
12-95	4.1	3.9	3.7	3.6	3.4	3.2	3.2	2.8	2.5	1.6	1.2	0.8	1.5	1.8	1.4	1.3	1.4	5.0		470.3
1-96	3.8	3.7	3.5	3.4	3.2	3.0	3.0	2.6	2.3	1.5	1.1	0.7	1.3	1.5	1.1	1.0	1.0	2.6	0.3	470.4
	6-94	7-94	8-94	9-94	10-94	11-94	12-94	1-95	2-95	3-95	4-95	5-95	6-95	7-95	8-95	9-95	10-95	11-95	12-95	

Source: Federal Reserve Bank of St. Louis (1996, p. 5).

155

Table 4. Money Stock (M2)
(Compound Annual Rates of Change)

Terminal Month	Initial Month																			Billions of Dollars
	6-94	7-94	8-94	9-94	10-94	11-94	12-94	1-95	2-95	3-95	4-95	5-95	6-95	7-95	8-95	9-95	10-95	11-95	12-95	
7-94	2.6																			3508.0
8-94	0.6	-1.3																		3504.1
9-94	0.4	0.7	-0.7																	3503.8
10-94	0.3	-0.5	-0.0	0.0																3503.9
11-94	0.4	-0.1	0.3	0.5	1.0															3506.8
12-94	0.5	0.1	0.5	0.6	0.9	0.9														3509.4
1-95	0.7	0.4	0.8	1.0	1.3	1.5	2.0													3515.3
2-95	0.7	0.5	0.8	0.9	1.2	1.2	1.4	0.8												3517.5
3-95	0.9	0.7	1.0	1.2	1.5	1.6	1.8	1.7	2.6											3525.1
4-95	1.3	1.1	1.4	1.6	1.9	2.1	2.4	2.5	3.4	4.2										3537.3
5-95	1.6	1.5	1.8	2.1	2.4	2.6	2.9	3.2	4.0	4.6	5.1									3551.9
6-95	2.3	2.3	2.7	3.0	3.4	3.7	4.2	4.7	5.7	6.7	7.9	10.9								3582.6
7-95	2.7	2.7	3.0	3.4	3.7	4.1	4.5	5.0	5.8	6.6	7.5	8.7	6.5							3601.5
8-95	3.0	3.0	3.4	3.7	4.0	4.4	4.8	5.2	6.0	6.7	7.3	8.1	6.7	6.9						3621.6
9-95	3.1	3.1	3.4	3.7	4.1	4.4	4.8	5.2	5.8	6.3	6.8	7.2	6.0	5.7	4.5					3635.0
10-95	3.0	3.0	3.4	3.6	3.9	4.2	4.6	4.8	5.4	5.8	6.0	6.2	5.1	4.6	3.4	2.4				3642.1
11-95	3.1	3.1	3.4	3.6	3.9	4.2	4.5	4.7	5.2	5.5	5.7	5.8	4.8	4.4	3.5	3.0	3.7			3653.2
12-95	3.2	3.2	3.5	3.8	4.1	4.3	4.6	4.8	5.2	5.5	5.7	5.8	5.0	4.6	4.1	3.9	4.7	5.8		3670.3
1-96	3.3	3.3	3.6	3.9	4.1	4.3	4.6	4.8	5.2	5.5	5.6	5.7	4.9	4.7	4.3	4.2	4.8	5.3	4.9	3685.0
	6-94	7-94	8-94	9-94	10-94	11-94	12-94	1-95	2-95	3-95	4-95	5-95	6-95	7-95	8-95	9-95	10-95	11-95	12-95	

Source: Federal Reserve Bank of St. Louis (1996, p. 5).

With increases in aggregate expenditures, the nominal value of GDP rises. Of course, it makes a great deal of difference if the increase is centered on increased output and employment or if the increase is primarily in the form of rising prices. There are no hard and fast rules for establishing the relative movements of output and prices. In an environment of relatively full employment and full capacity utilization, increases in aggregate expenditures will impact more heavily on prices than if the economy is in a downturn or just emerging from a recession. The rate of growth of aggregate expenditures is also relevant. In an economic situation like that of 1996, with capacity utilization rates relatively high and with low levels of unemployment, the moderate rate of growth of aggregate expenditures is less inflationary than if expenditures and output were increasing more rapidly.

A useful rule of thumb is that historically for the United States real GDP has increased at an annual rate of slightly less than 3 percent. Of course, expansion and contraction phases of the business cycle generate rates both higher and lower than the mean. The degree to which expansions increase output above 3 percent will help to determine the inflationary pressures that develop and the subsequent slowdown in economic activity. Moderate expansions will be less inflationary and are likely to lead to more moderate downturns. The economy corrects its excesses, and the severity of corrections is tied closely to the severity of the excesses that precede them. Adjusting the historical average to take into account phases of the business cycle will allow for an estimate of real GDP growth in response to increases in aggregate expenditures.

Changes in the availability of money are the best predictors of price changes. Six month trends in the monetary base and *M2* provide a reasonable forecast of the behavior of aggregate spending over the subsequent nine to twelve months. When the monetary base and M2 change there is a time lag until the full effects on total spending work their way throughout the economy. Bank reserves are lent and relent, and the spending generated by the turnover of money is time consuming. It is reasonable to expect that most of the effects on GDP will be experienced over the next 12-month period. Thus, Federal Reserve policy actions during 1995 are the policies that explain GDP behavior in 1996.

V. INTEREST RATES

Federal Reserve policies have an immediate impact on short-term interest rates. Expanding or contracting the availability of bank reserves causes the federal funds rate and rates on other short-term financial instruments to change instantly. When the Federal Reserve announces it is raising or lowering interest rates by 1/8 or 1/4 percent, it is the very short end of the credit markets where it has its predictable influence. The announcement by the Federal Reserve that it intends to lower rates is accomplished through its open market operations. By making open market purchases, reserves are injected into the banking system and the Federal funds rate will be impacted immediately. If the cost of borrowing reserves falls, changes in the prime rate may or may not occur, depending on the extent of the change in the federal funds rate and whether or not the change is interpreted to be part of a trend in rates. In this way, the Federal Reserve can have an effect on bank variable lending and savings rates.

One result of the Federal Reserve actions to reduce short-term interest rates is an increase in the monetary base and subsequently the money supply. Simultaneously, interest rate declines may encourage business and individual borrowing and expenditures, and with more money in the system, total expenditures will rise directly. The opposite will be true for periods of contractionary policy. Bank reserves will be reduced or increased more slowly, short-term rates will tend to rise, and the cut back in the availability of reserves will reduce bank lending and the expansion of money. Total expenditures will fall or rise less rapidly. Increases in reserves reduce short-term rates, and *vice versa*. The effects on long-term rates are more ambiguous. Long-term rates are less influenced by the immediate effect of changes in the monetary base than by the market perceptions of the long-term effects on economic activity, and particularly on inflation. Long-term interest rates embody inflationary expectations as one component. If the rate of inflation is expected to increase, long-term rates will increase; lenders will ask for higher interest rates to compensate for the reduced purchasing power that repayments will represent. For similar reasons, borrowers willingly will pay a premium with expected inflation.

It is improper to generalize about the effects of Federal Reserve policies on interest rates. A statement that "The Federal Reserve raised (lowered) interest rates by tightening (loosening) monetary policy" is misleading. A tightening may result in an increase in short-term rates, but if this tightening dampens inflationary expectations because the amount of money and aggregate expenditures might fall, intermediate and/or long-term rates may decline. From the perspective of an individual business, the effects of Federal Reserve policy must be judged by the terms of its own borrowed funds. Variable rates tied to prime rates of banks or to the London Inter-Bank Overnight Rate (LIBOR) will move up immediately in response to Federal Reserve tightening, but over a longer time horizon anti-inflationary monetary policy will keep these rates lower than a more expansionary monetary policy, and long-term rates may decline, not rise. A useful way to study the behavior of short-term rates relative to long-term rates is in the behavior of yield curves. A yield curve is a plot of the yields on securities with different terms to maturity.

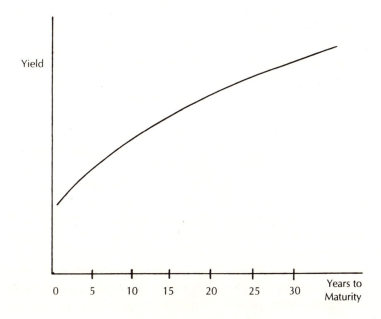

Figure 1.

A "normal" yield curve is one with a positive slope. That is, yields increase as the maturity period lengthens. The explanations for this slope can be quite sophisticated (Auerbach, 1988). For the purpose of this chapter, two considerations are primary. First, long term lenders may want a liquidity premium to be compensated for the risk of longer-term loans. Second, investors may anticipate that short-term rates are likely to rise in the future, and long-term rates will increase now in response to these expectations.

What would be the effects of the Federal Reserve draining reserves from the banking system and raising short-term rates? At the short-end of the maturity scale, yields would tend to rise. But if this decrease in the monetary base and the supply of money is judged to reduce the potential for inflation over the longer term, long-term yields may fall or rise less than short-term rates. The yield curve would flatten. The yield curve might become more steep in the opposite situation. An expansionary policy by the Federal Reserve that increases the money supply might be judged to have potential inflationary effects, and long-term rates may rise relative to short-term rates. The yield curve would be steeper. Thus, the yield curve can offer insight into the market perceptions of future interest rates and inflationary pressures. Published daily in *The Wall Street Journal* near the Credit Markets column, one can compare the yield curves at three- or six-month intervals to gauge inflationary expectations and potential movements in interest rates.

The experience during 1994 is instructive. Over the period from May 1994 to February 1995 the discount rates increased from 3.5 percent to 5.25 percent as the Federal Reserve slowed the growth of the monetary base and *M2*. The effects on the yield curves for three different dates is shown in Figure 2.

At the short end, yields increased. But the yield curves subsequently flattened, and the yield on long-term securities declined substantially by the end of 1995. These changes suggest that market perceptions were that the potential for future inflation had diminished. To have characterized the changes that occurred in Federal Reserve policy over this nine-month period as one of raising interest rates is over simplified and somewhat misleading. For businesses that borrow at longer maturities, the principal effect may have been to lower the costs of funds.

Percent, weekly averages

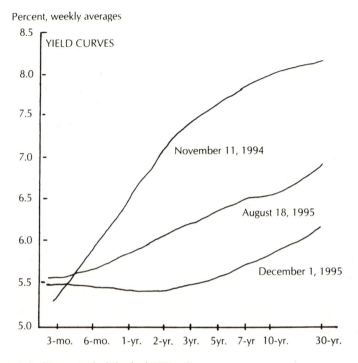

Source: Federal Reserve Bank of Cleveland (1995, p. 2).

Figure 2. Yield Curves, 11/94 - 12/95

Fundamentally, all inflations are a monetary phenomena. Shocks to the system, as exemplified by the fourfold increase in the price of crude oil back in 1973-1974 can move prices up on a one time basis, but substantial oil price increases can not cause inflation unless subsequent monetary policies ratify and magnify the change. The 12.2 percent rate of inflation in 1974 was not caused by OPEC but rather by U.S. dismantling of price controls and expansionary monetary policies. The moderate rates of inflation in Japan and Germany at that time are not consistent with a premise that OPEC was the inflationary villain. By itself, a substantial increase in the price of oil would be offset by deflationary effects in other segments of the economy as expenditures were diverted from other sectors to purchases of oil and to segments of the economy where oil is an important input.

V. THE INTERNATIONAL SECTOR

United States international payments (the supply of U.S. dollars into international markets) result from United States imports of goods and services and U.S. financial investments abroad. On the other side of the ledger, United States international receipts (the demand for U.S. dollars in international markets) are generated by U.S. exports of goods and services and foreign financial investments in the United States. Imports and exports of goods and services are measured in the current account of the U.S. international balance of payments; financial investments, both short-term and long-term, are accounted for in the capital account. When all international transactions are included, U.S. international payments must be equal to U.S. international receipts. This equality is established by allowing the value of the U.S. dollar in international markets to respond to the supply and demand for U.S. dollars (a fluctuating exchange rate system). In a competitive market for apples, price fluctuates in response to supply-demand conditions and price clears the market. The amount offered at the competitive price equals the amount buyers are willing and able to purchase. The same is true in the international market for U.S. dollars. The value of the U.S. dollar fluctuates in response to supply-demand conditions and clears the market such that U.S. total international receipts equal its total international payments. The term, "balance of international payments deficit," would indicate that U.S. international payments exceed U.S. international receipts: therefore, it cannot describe the international balance of payments position of the United States. For the United States, deficits and surpluses in its international balance of payments did exist prior to 1971 at a time when the United States maintained a fixed exchange rate. In the analogy to the apple market, a fixed price imposed on the market for apples can cause shortages or surpluses of apples. Price movements that respond to supply and demand eliminate shortages and surpluses.

It is possible, of course, to have a surplus or deficit for any subset of international transactions. If one looks at the merchandise trade account, U.S. imports of merchandise regularly exceed its exports of merchandise. This deficit on merchandise account is referred to as the trade deficit. On the other hand, U.S. imports of services typically are less than exports of services, and the United States has an export surplus on international services. Combining both merchandise and services measures the balance on current account. For 1994, the amounts were:

	Imports	*Exports*
Merchandise	$669 billion	$502 billion
Services	$139 billion	$199 billion
Total	$808 billion	$701 billion
Net balance	$107 billion	

Combining these two accounts, there is a net deficit of $107 billion, and for the current account, U.S. international payments exceed its international receipts. But in addition to movements of goods and services, there are substantial financial investments (the capital account of the international balance of payments). For 1994, foreign investments in the United States increased by $291 billion (receipts) while U.S. assets abroad increased by $125 billion (payments) (U.S. Department of Commerce, 1995, p. 66). Thus, on capital account, U.S. international receipts exceeded international payments by $166 billion. Comparing the net payments on merchandise and services of $107 billion with the net receipts on capital account of $166 billion results in net receipts of $59 billion. This $59 billion is offset by U.S. government aid, U.S. pension payments, and U.S. private remittances abroad, totalling $36 billion, a statistical discrepancy (inaccurate statistics) of net payments of $14 billion, and net payments of $9 billion of investment income. When all transactions are accounted for, international payments equal international receipts. To summarize:

1994 (billions of dollars)

	International Payments	*International Receipts*
Merchandise	669	502
Services	139	199
Investment income	147	138
Unilateral Transfers	36	
Foreign Investment	125	291
Statistical Discrepancy	14	
	1,130	1,130

Because total U.S. international payments must equal total international receipts, transactions on current account are inextricably linked to those on the capital account. The net inflow of international investment funds into the United States is both caused by the deficit on the current account *and* causes the deficit on current account.

Too often the causation is viewed in only one direction. This approach implies that international financial investments are induced by the net transactions on current account. The reasoning is that since U.S. imports of goods and services exceed exports of goods and services, net international payments supply U.S. dollars to foreigners who then invest the funds in U.S. financial markets. This may have been a reasonable approach 30 or 40 years ago when world financial markets were less integrated and less dynamic. Under present conditions, however, it is as reasonable to start with the assertion that the United States has developed a comparative advantage in the exporting of financial assets. The size and relative stability of U.S. financial markets, the political stature of the United States, and the openness of American financial markets all combine to attract foreign investors. It also explains the role of the U.S. dollar as the world's primary money. Over time, the only way that the United States can export more financial assets than it imports is to import more goods and services than it exports. Foreigners must earn the dollars they desire to invest in the United States on current account transactions. The popular view that the U.S. trade deficit is "unfavorable" ignores the total picture of U.S. international transactions. In many respects, the trade deficit and the net exports of financial assets is quite advantageous to the United States. The relatively low rates of saving in the United States is augmented by foreign saving, and the inflow of foreign investment funds keeps interest rates lower in this country and promotes productive investment. The exportation of financial assets has the additional advantage of not being an intensive user of natural resources, nor is it a polluting industry.

The role of international financial investors in the United States is substantial. By the end of 1995 foreign assets in the United States were approximately $2 trillion (U.S. Department of Commerce,

1995, p. 77). Approximately 16 percent of the gross public debt of the U.S. Treasury, or $785 billion, is owned by foreigners (Board of Governors of the Federal Reserve System, 1996, p. A30). Foreign investors net purchases of Treasury coupon securities in 1995 amounted to $140 billion. Private foreign investors accounted for 70 percent of the total, with the remainder being bought by foreign central banks and other official institutions (*Wall Street Journal, 1996, April 8*). Also, foreign direct (ownership) investment in the United States is almost $800 billion (U.S. Department of Commerce, 1995, p. 54). Finally, at the end of 1995, U.S. banks reported liabilities to foreigners of $1.1 trillion. At the same time, U.S. banks had claims on foreigners of $519 billion (Board of Governors of the Federal Reserve System, 1996, p. A.30).

These statistics illustrate the size and importance of the role of international financial transactions. The Federal Reserve must be alert to the impact of its policies on international investment and how movements of foreign funds into the United States will impact on interest rates and aggregate expenditures in this country. However, while consideration for these effects makes the conduct of Federal Reserve policy more complicated, it does not alter the abilities of the Federal Reserve authorities to exercise their influence on the performance of the U.S. economy. What is obvious is that all companies, mid-size or not, whether they actively import or export, are part of a global market for investment capital. Lenders seek the best risk adjusted rates of return world wide, and the sources of funds are global. The global economy is more pronounced in financial markets than in any other aspect of economic activity. In a sense all companies worldwide are in direct competition with each other for investment capital.

VI. SUMMARY AND CONCLUSIONS

Managers and owners of mid-size businesses will find it to their advantage to attempt forecasts of national economic activity. Trends in GDP, prices, employment, and interest rates constitute the backdrop for decisions of individual businesses with their own product mix and industry specific conditions, problems, and prospects. Economic forecasts are available in the general financial and economics press, but unless the reader has some basis for independent judgment, it is difficult to assess these forecasts, especially when there are substantial differences of opinion about the direction of the U.S. economy.

The information required to make these judgments is readily available and does not require a major time commitment. Sources such as *The Wall Street Journal*, *Barron's*, and a few publications from the Federal Reserve System provide adequate information. The recommended Federal Reserve publications are *Economic Trends*, from the Federal Reserve Bank of Cleveland, and *Monetary Trends*, published by the Federal Reserve Bank of St. Louis. Establishing trends by looking at data every three to six months can provide the information that fits into the approach suggested by this analysis.

The limitations of the analysis should be recognized. It provides a forecast of broad trends in the economy but does not attempt any degree of precision. Professional forecasts are made to the tenth of a percentage point, but professional forecasts are revised frequently, typically each quarter. Is the owner of a business any better off with a forecast of GDP growth of 2.4 percent compared with one that expects an increase of GDP between 2 and 3 percent? For most, the latter probably will suffice.

Under conditions of substantial inflation or a major recession, the basic analysis here will be less useful. Under these conditions the velocity of money becomes more unpredictable and influential. In these circumstances the impact on aggregate expenditures and GDP of changes in the monetary base and the money supply will be more difficult to predict. Finally, the analysis, like all forecasts, is not helpful in anticipating major shocks to the system such as regional conflicts, major financial upheavals, or disruptions to normal commerce such as the OPEC boycott of oil deliveries to the United States during the early 1970s. Nor can it predict the policy responses to these events in Washington, D.C.

Recognizing these limitations, what forecast would a nonprofessional make about economic activity in 1996? The monetary base increased by 4.1 percent from June 1994 through December 1995. The comparable figures for *M2* is 3.3 percent. For the last half of 1995, the monetary base increased by only 1.5 percent, while *M2* increased by 5 percent. GDP growth in 1995 was less than 2 percent, and the rate of inflation as measured by the consumer price index ranged between 2.5 percent and 3 percent. The slow rate of growth of the monetary base in the last half of 1995 suggests that any increase in *M2* during 1996 will be moderate. With anticipated steady but moderate growth in aggregate expenditures, it is reasonable to forecast a continuation of moderate increases in real GDP of between 2 and 3 percent and a rate of inflation of less than 3 percent. With the federal funds rate approximating 5.5 percent at the end of 1995, down slightly from nearly 5.75 percent earlier in the year, it appears that the availability of bank reserves is consistent with moderate increases in the federal funds rate, but in the absence of new inflationary pressures, interest rates in general should not increase substantially during 1996. The basic structure of U.S. international payments and receipts in early 1996 remains the same; a current account deficit is counterbalanced by a surplus on capital account. Financial markets in the United States remain relatively strong, and that, plus the relative strength of the U.S. dollar in international markets, suggests foreign financial inflows into the United States will remain strong and will help in restraining interest rate increases.

"Bond Prices Plummet Because of Inflation Fears As Key Commodity Index Hits Eight-Year High." This headline of the Credit Markets column in *The Wall Street Journal* on April 11, 1996 reflects investor fears of renewed inflation. How should an owner-manager of a mid-size business interpret this news? The analysis of this article suggests that inflationary pressures in the U.S. economy are muted. An understanding of the longer term trends can provide perspective to the daily headlines that appear in the press. Does this basic analysis provide the right perspective? The proof of the pudding is in the eating.

NOTES

1. Of course, professional forecasts are available and some are discussed regularly in publications such as *The Wall Street Journal*. The problem is that much of the reporting of forecasts presents contrasting views, and the nonprofessional and those who don't have adequate time to study the reasons for these differences often do not find them useful.
2. The term "federal funds" has nothing to do with the federal government. The funds are transferred using the Federal Reserve wire transfer system.
3. Federal Reserve Bank of St. Louis, Post Office Box 442, St. Louis, MO 63166.

REFERENCES

Auerbach, R.D. (1988). *Money, banking, and financial markets* (3rd Ed., pp. 249-260). New York: Macmillan.
Barron's Market Week. (1996, April 1). Money supply table, p. 101.
Board of Governors of the Federal Reserve System. (1996). *Federal reserve bulletin, 82*(2), A8, A30, A97.
Federal Reserve Bank of St. Louis. (1996, March). *Monetary trends*, pp. 5, 7.
Fisher, I. (1963). *The purchasing power of money, its determination and relation to credit, interest, and crisis.* New York: August M. Kelley.
Friedman, M. (1956). The quantity theory of money: A restatement. In M. Freidman (Ed.), *Studies in the quantity, theory of money.* Chicago, IL: University of Chicago Press.
Friedman, M. (1969). Factors affecting the level of interest rates. In United States Savings and Loan League, *Proceedings of a Conference on Savings and Residential Financing* (pp. 11-17). Chicago, IL: United States Savings and Loan League.
Friedman, M., & Schwartz, A. (1970). *Monetary statistics of the United States.* New York: Columbia University Press.
Friedman, M., & Schwartz, A. (1963). *A monetary history of the United States, 1867-1960.* Princeton, NJ: Princeton University Press.
Mishkin, F.S. (1995). *The economics of money, banking, and financial markets* (4th Ed., pp. 544-565). New York: HarperCollins.
U.S. Department of Commerce. (1995a). *Survey of current business, 75*(8). U.S. Department of Commerce. (1995a). *Survey of current business, 75*(11/12).
The Wall Street Journal. Various issues.

ABOUT THE AUTHORS

James Alm is a Professor of Economics at the University of Colorado at Boulder. He earned his master's degree from the University of Chicago and his doctorate at the University of Wisconsin at Madison. He has also taught at Syracuse University in the Maxwell School of Citizenship and Public Affairs.

Professor Alm teaches and conducts research in the area of public economics (the study of government taxation and expenditures). Much of his research has examined the responses of individuals and firms to taxation in such areas as the tax treatment of the family, privatization, the line item veto, social security, housing, indexation and tax and expenditure limitations. He is especially known for his work on tax compliance.

Alm has also worked extensively on fiscal reforms overseas, including projects in Bangladesh, Indonesia, Jamaica, Turkey, Egypt, Hungary, China, the Philippines and the Russian Federation. He has been a member of advisory committees to the Governor and the General Assembly of the State of Colorado on health care and tax reform issues, and is currently on the editorial board of the *National Tax Journal and Public Finance Quarterly*.

R. Glenn Hubbard is a Russell L. Carson Professor of Economics and Finance at the Graduate School of Business at Columbia University. He received his Ph.D. in economics at Harvard University, where he received National Science Foundation and Alfred P. Sloan Foundation fellowships. He began his academic career at Northwestern University in 1983, moving to Columbia University in 1988.

Hubbard served as Deputy Assistant Secretary (Tax Analysis) of the U.S. Treasury Department during the Bush Administration. He also served as a visiting professor at Harvard University and the University of Chicago and a John M. Olin Fellow at the National Bureau of Economic Research, where he remains a research associate in programs on public economics, monetary economics, corporate finance, economic fluctuations, and industrial organization.

Hubbard has published numerous articles in public finance, financial economics, macroeconomics, industrial organization, energy economics, and public policy. He has been a research consultant for the Federal Reserve Board, Federal Reserve Bank of New York, the Internal Revenue Service, the Social Security Administration, the U.S. Department of the Treasury, the U.S. International Trade Commission, the National Science Foundation, and the World Bank.

Gary D. Libecap is Anheuser-Busch professor and directs the Karl Eller Center at the University of Arizona where he is professor of economics and law. He also is a research associate with the National Bureau of Economic Research. He received his Ph.D. and M.A. from the University of Pennsylvania and B.A. from the University of Montana. He was an Olin Fellow at the California Institute of Technology and the University of Southern California Law Center, and was a Fulbright lecturer in Montevideo, Uruguay. Libecap has authored, coauthored, or edited thirteen books, including *The Federal Civil Service System and the Problem of Bureaucracy: The Economics and Politics of Institutional Change* with Ronald Johnson, and *The Political Economy of Regulation: An Historical Analysis of Government and the Economy*, coedited with Claudia Goldin. He is coeditor of *The Journal of Economic History*.

Jonathan R. Macey is the J. DuPratt White Professor of Law at Cornell University and Director of the John M. Olin Program in Law and Economics at Cornell Law School. Professor Macey is a graduate of Harvard College and the Yale Law School. Prior to entering legal education, he clerked on the U.S. Court of

Appeals for the Second Circuit. He has taught at the law schools of Emory University, the University of Virginia, the University of Chicago, the University of Toronto, the University of Tokyo and the Stockholm School of Economics. He also has been a Research Fellow at the International Center for Economic Research in Turin, Italy.

James F. Smith, known for his accuracy as well as his sense of humor, was just named the best overall economic forecaster in the country by *The Wall Street Journal*. He is a finance professor at the Kenan-Flagler School of Business at the University of North Carolina at Chapel Hill (UNC) and the author of Kenan-Flagler's bimonthly "Business Forecast." Smith received his B.A., and Ph.D. degrees, all in economics, from Southern Methodist University.

Smith has over 25 years of experience as an economic forecaster. He served 11 years on the board of the National Association of Business Economists (NABE) and as president of the organization. In 1992 he headed the NABE delegation to China. He also serves on the board of directors of the National Bureau of Economic Research (NBER).

Smith's private sector experience includes employment as the chief economist at Union Carbide Corp., and at Sears, Roebuck & Co. Where he was director of credit research. He was a senior economist for the Federal Reserve Board and a member of President Reagan's Council of Economic Advisors.

Murray Weidenbaum has been an economist in three worlds— business, government and academia. He holds the Mallinckrodt Distinguished University Professorship at Washington University in St. Louis, where he also serves as director of the Center for the Study of American Business. Weidenbaum received a B.B.A. from City College of New York, an M.A. from Columbia University and a Ph.D. from Princeton University.

He is known for his research on economic policy, taxes, government spending, and regulation. *Business and Government in the Global Marketplace* is the most recent of his seven books.

He has written several hundred articles in publications ranging from the *American Economic Review* to *The Wall Street Journal.*

In the early 1980s Weidenbaum was President Reagan's first chairman of the Council of Economic Advisers. In that capacity he helped to formulate the economic policy of the Reagan Administration and was a key spokesman for the Administration on economic and financial issues. From 1982-1989 he was a member of the President's Economic Policy Advisory Board.

Weidenbaum's international activities include serving as Chairman of the Economic Policy Committee of the Organization for Economic Cooperation and Development. He received the National Order of Merit from France in recognition of his contributions to foreign policy.

Donald A. Wells is a Professor of Economics at the University of Arizona. He earned his master's degree from the University of Virginia and his doctorate at University of Oregon.

He began his academic career at Southern Illinois University in 1960, and joined the University of Arizona in 1969.

Professor Wells teaches economics education, economic development and international economics. His primary research interests are experimental economics as a teaching tool and international finance. He has received The University of Arizona Foundation Leicester and Kathryn Sherrill Creative Teaching Award and Business and Public Administration College Outstanding Undergraduate Faculty Teaching Award.

Wells has published articles in experimental economics, Saudia Arabian development and international finance. He teaches in executive development programs and has conducted NSF sponsored seminars for economic faculty.

Advances in the Study of Entrepreneurship, Innovation, and Economic Growth

Edited by **Gary D. Libecap**, *Director,*
Karl Eller Center, University of Arizona

Volume 8, In preparation, Winter 1996
ISBN 1-55938-703-0 Approx. $73.25

TENTATIVE CONTENTS: Introduction: The 1996 University of Arizona/Finova Forum: A Dialogue Addressing Political and Economic Factors Affecting Mid-Size Business, *Gary D. Libecap.* The Overlooked Middle: Government Regulation and Mid-Size Business, *Murray Weidenbaum.* Mid-Size Business, Rule-Making Theory, and Litigation Reform: Beware Congressmen Bearing Gifts, *Jonathan R. Macey.* Fiscal Policies and Mid-Size Business, *James Alm.* An Analysis of the Potential Impacts of Federal Government Budgetary Restraints on Mid-Size Business Firms in the United States, *James F. Smith.* Understanding a Consumption Tax as Fundamental Tax Reform, *R. Glenn Hubbard.* Forecasting U.S. Economic Trends for Use by Mid-Size Business: The Role of the Federal Reserve, *Donald A. Wells.*

Also Available:
Volumes 1-7 (1986-1996)
  + Supplement 1 (1989) $73.25 each

JAI PRESS INC.
55 Old Post Road No. 2 - P.O. Box 1678
Greenwich, Connecticut 06836-1678
Tel: (203) 661- 7602   Fax: (203) 661-0792

J A I   P R E S S

Advances in the Economic Analysis of Participatory and Labor-Managed Firms

Edited by **Derek C. Jones,** *Department of Economics, Hamilton College and* **Jan Svejnar,** *Department of Economics, University of Pittsburgh, and Cerge, Charles University, Prague*

Volume 6, Public Policy and the Management of Innovation in Technology-Based Entrepreneurship
1996, 260 pp. $73.25
ISBN 0-7623-0004-3